FLUKE

FLUKE

An Angler's Guide

Bob Sampson, Jr.

Burford Books

Printed in the United States of America.

10   9   8   7   6   5   4   3   2   1

Library of Congress Cataloging-in-Publication Data
    Sampson, Bob.
    Fluke / Bob Sampson, Jr.
            p.   cm.
    Includes index.
    ISBN 1-58080-128-5 (pbk.)
    1. Flatfish fishing.   I. Title.

SH691.F5S26   2005
799.17'69—dc22
                                2004028149

Contents

FOREWORD

My first encounter with a fluke was a complete "fluke."

That summer, our family vacation was spent in what we used to call "the way back" of Groton Long Point, in Groton, Connecticut. Out of sight from the high-priced beach houses on the ocean side of this wealthy summer community was a row of tiny rental cottages. "Cute and clean," as my mother put it, our place was flanked by a mosquito-infested tidal creek full of nasty, ill tempered blue crabs that provided enough adventure to keep a ten-year-old busy for a week.

I spent hours walking that creek, checking baited crab lines and scooping up any crabs that had been attracted. At the time I didn't like eating them, but my dad and his pal Don Oat would pay me a quarter for every one I could catch. In the long run it amounted to about a dollar per quart for the blood I lost handling those things. It seemed a fair trade off at the time.

A week on the ocean was in itself quite an experience for a developing young outdoorsman, high adventure in the first degree. At that point all of my fishing had been done in freshwater, with the exception of a few, mostly unsuccessful striper trips, which amounted to tossing Gibbs Poppers into the surf off Crowell's Point, a great, tide-swept rocky point near the center of Groton Long Point. Long-time family friends lived there and as I grew up, they graciously allowed me access to the ocean through their property to fish, for the price of an occasional blackfish fillet.

Each day my mom and I would take a walk to one of the swimming beaches from which I would explore the coast. Even as a kid I never spent time laying on the beach, instead spending my days seeking out what there was to catch around the nearby rocks.

On one of my exploratory walks from the beach with a friend, who knew the point, we walked down the street to "East Dock," an impressive structure that seemed to stretch a mile out into the ocean, although in reality it was about 25 yards of splintering, aging pier.

The next day I brought along one of my freshwater spinning rigs to do some fishing with a basic sandworm and sinker rig. For about two hours of fishing the dropping tide, I had a couple of cunners, a porgy, and a blowfish to show for my efforts. At one point I decided to move from the end of the pier to a different spot half way down, so I could cast towards some rocks that began showing as the tide dropped. Just as I began reeling the rig in to check the bait, it suddenly got heavy and stopped. Thinking I was snagged, I leaned into the dead weight—and felt a "flop-flop" at the other end.

After a little heave-hauling and walking the fish down the pier and along some rocks to a place where I could reach it with the trout net that I had brought along, I had a decent fluke that nearly filled the net. I had no clue what it was. At that point in my angling career I had only caught blubbery lipped winter flounder on sand worms and had only seen fluke fillets my dad would occasionally bring home from the trips he made with a couple of his buddies from work.

I was looking at my catch and pondering whether or not I should let it go when my mom showed up to retrieve me for lunch. She knew what I had and immediately took possession of it for dinner.

It was a very unimpressive experience for me as an angler, because I was more interested in striped bass and bluefish—a passion that still burns within me to this day. But it was a start on a sideline of fishing that has grown to account for a large portion of the time I spend on the ocean every summer.

After getting a driver's license, which allowed me and my fishing buddies to expand our horizons from the bass and trout ponds that we could reach with our bicycles, we began catching stripers and blues on a regular basis with a life-long friend, Captain Gil Liepold, now of Gil Liepold & Associates (his yacht brokerage firm) whose family rented another of those cottages along "the way back" at Groton Long Point.

I met Gil in Frau Von Schlippe's Deutch Class in high school. Our friendship developed from a common interest in the outdoors, a friendship that began over a pheasant-hunting trip in our freshman year. Along with a couple of other friends who had similar interests, we all forged a friendship that is as strong today as adults, with grown children, as it was when we were sporting around in high school and college.

Gil had a 17-foot wooden boat moored a short, wet wade out from their cottage, in which we ran all over the eastern end of Long Island Sound pursuing striped bass, bluefish and occasionally stopping along the rocks on the south side of Fishers Island to spear some blackfish for the grill.

In those testosterone-filled early years of fishing the ocean, there was no time to fish for dull, small, non-drag-pulling fluke. In fact, I used to get pissed when Gil would stop the boat to make a drift or two for fluke to appease his mom. (In those days a random drift or two was all it would take to catch a couple of eaters.) She frequently bribed us, with a "gas money for fluke deal," that we were pretty much obliged to fulfill when ever she asked. In those days, it didn't take very long to catch a couple of fluke, so it was never much of an imposition despite the fact that I initially considered this species to be a waste of precious striper-fishing time.

A decade later, with a broadening of my angling horizons and a young family that liked to eat fish, fluke fishing took on a new meaning. I had been out on a targeted fluke trip with a couple of friends from work. We caught a ton of fish, including some 4- to 6-pounders and ended up with a batch of fillets that would make anybody happy.

They were so tasty that I invested the time to learn where and how to catch fluke around what were then my home fishing grounds in the Mystic, Noank area. I would launch my 14-foot Lund at Shaffer's Marina and fish the fertile fluke waters from Mystic and Groton Long Point east to Stonington or Napatree Point, occasionally dropping out to the south side of Fishers Island or Misquamicut Beach when conditions were flat calm.

Those days were fun and adventurous. I would often have my young kids along fluking with small, light rods tailored for their small hands and body size. Somewhere in the boat there would always be (and still is) a spinning rod armed with poppers, swimming plugs or soft plastics to toss at any striped bass or blues that might show themselves during the course of a trip.

The final component in my development into a fluke fan took place a few years later. From the beginning, I had been taught to fish with classic fluke drift rigs, which are a sinker with leader, hook and good-sized Colorado-style spinner blades in front of the hook to attract the fish. Most were fished with a two- to four- ounce sinker, on a short, pool-cue rod and level wind reel, which was totally "dead" feeling and not terribly enjoyable to fish with—but it worked.

That all changed when a college kid, "J.R.", John Roy took a job for me as a seasonal worker on the recreational fisheries program that I headed for the Connecticut DEP. J.R. had grown up in Noank and worked weekends on a charter boat that did a good deal of fluke fishing. He knew his stuff and was always fun to fish with.

Early in our association, he took me and another biologist to fish the waters off Mystic, primarily to do some drifting for fluke on a beautiful July day. The plan was to fish for fluke during the heat of the day, then switch over to stripers as the sun set, a strategy I frequently employ to this day to make for a more enjoyable and varied outing.

My buddy and I broke out those big clunky rods, with classic drift rigs and baited up. J.R. pulled out a small bucktail, tied it on a light spinning rod added a couple strips of squid and immediately began to bail the fluke. After his fifth or sixth fish, to our combined nothing, he asked if we wanted to "try a jig." A double head shake, two knots later with jigs now attached to our spinning rods and we were all nailing fluke on nearly every drift.

That was all that was needed to turn me into a fluke fanatic, a fun and effective light-tackle method to catch these good-tasting and (in their own way) sporty and challenging fish.

That was about thirty years ago. I have been trying to perfect and improve on this basic fluke jigging method ever since. Like skinning the proverbial cat, there is more than one way to catch a fluke. Some rigging methods are better than others under certain conditions. But part of the beauty in fluking is the fact that about anything you do that is within certain reasonable parameters will catch fluke. If you don't do things right, you won't hook up, even when you are right on top of them.

Jay Piacienze holds up a 5-pounder caught during the spring run off Misquamicut Beach, a time when the fluking is easy every year.

Today fluke fishing is one of the things I most look forward to every spring. Most years, I put as much time into targeting and fishing for fluke as any other single marine species.

There is no real mystery to catching fluke—it is a bottom species that is not really hard to locate or catch. However, by paying attention and fine-tuning tackle, rigging and angling techniques, this style of fishing can be made much more enjoyable and productive. And by learning a few basic tactics to locate fluke, the rigging and fishing methods that will get them to strike, anyone's catch can be dramatically increased.

Fluke or summer flounder have always been a favorite among marine fishermen, especially the commercial sector, for their flaky, white, delicately flavored fillets. Sport fishermen have always taken their share of the annual catch throughout the range of this popular fish, which has become even more of a favorite with the advent of light tackle fishing methods.

Fluke fishing is popular for many reasons. First, they are an inshore species that can be caught from a dock, jetty, surf, or boat. Fluke don't require highly sophisticated tackle, gear, or rigging techniques. Once a good spot has been "dialed in," it can be easy to catch large numbers—one reason this species took it in the face during the days of "non-management" of marine species.

Fluke are a great bottom species that the whole family can learn to catch with regularity. You don't have to get up early or fish after dark to be successful at catching these fish. They are a "bankers hours species" that, providing the winds and tides are aligned properly, can be caught any time during the day when the tides are moving, and occasionally when they aren't.

As with any type of fishing, persistence is the key to success.

1

FLUKE, THE BIOLOGY OF A STEALTH PREDATOR

DESCRIPTION

Paralicthys dentatus is the scientific name for summer flounder, flatfish, or fluke as they are most commonly called throughout their range. Roughly translated this means something like, "the almost-fish with plenty of teeth," referring to its odd, flat shape and serious dentition. In the case of fluke, the *dentatus* or toothy handle is very appropriate, because they have a mouth full of sharp teeth designed to grab, damage and hold prey.

Fluke can be most easily identified by the fact that it is a "left handed flounder," in that looked at from above and facing in the same direction, its mouth is along the left side of its body, as opposed to the winter flounder which has its small, toothless mouth on the right side of its body. Fluke adults also have a rounded, nearly double-concave shape to their tails.

Windowpane flounder, or sand dabs, also have a left-sided mouth but have no teeth, and are much more square in shape and are nearly transparent, as their name implies.

The closest relative to fluke is another toothy, left-mouthed flounder called a four spot flounder (*Paralicthys oblongus*), a smaller cousin from the south that is distinguished by four dark spots on its dark side. It doesn't grow to much more than 16 or 18 inches in length.

Summer flounder coloration is typical of most flatfish in that they are dark on top and white on the bottom, with both eyes on the dark side. Their color is quite variable and in fact changes with the bottom background. According to Bigelow and Shroeder's *Fishes of the Gulf of Maine*, fluke change their patterns more than their actual coloration, tending to match the pattern of the background rather than its exact color. Flounder that are uniform brown to sandy tan in color have usually been caught from a smooth mud or sand bottom. Those taken from a rocky or gravel bottom will have dark and light "eye" spots that allow them to hide against any back ground.

Occasionally anglers will catch fish with all-dark bottoms, splotchy bottoms, even white spilling over on to the dark side. These are minor genetic variations that sometimes show in catches along the coast. The technical description for fluke is just that—technical. Suffice it to say any left-mouthed, toothy flatfish with two eyes on the same side of the head, with a flat space between the eyes, and that does not have four brown or dark spots on its body, is a fluke. There are only five other species of flatfish that are commonly caught in the shallow waters of the northeast. They include yellowtail flounder (a deep water species), winter flounder (commonly caught during cold weather), four spot flounder (occasional catches during summer), windowpane flounder (often caught mixed with fluke), and the tiny hogchoker (which looks like an oval sneaker sole with a border of fins). Hogchokers are seldom caught on hook and line due to their extremely weak and tiny mouths. In the south, from Florida to the Gulf of Mexico and beyond, the gulf flounder (*Paralicthys albigutta*) and southern flounder (*Paralicthys lethostigma*) replace the fluke in shallow waters of this region. The gulf flounder can be distinguished by three distinct dark, light-rimmed spots on its back. The southern flounder has diffused dark blotches and spots along its top, not to be confused with the circular, bull's-eye spots found on summer flounder to the north.

RANGE AND MIGRATION

Fluke range from southern Nova Scotia and the Gulf of Maine, south to the Carolinas and northern Florida, according to Bigelow and Shroeder. I have personally caught fluke to four and a half pounds from saltwater ponds around the golf communities at Hilton Head in South Carolina. Another time while fishing near the mouth of the inland waterway south of Disney World, a partner and I each caught fluke that were in the 4- to 5-pound range while fishing with live pinfish that were intended for school tarpon. Still, the heart of the fluke range is from the mid-Atlantic area north to Cape Cod, with some fish filtering north of there.

Summer flounder, as their name implies, prefer warmer waters between 56 degrees F, to 72 degrees F, with their optimum temperature around 66 degrees F, according to Gary Soucie's *Hook, Line and Sinker*.

To avoid winter chilling, fluke tend to move south and off shore to the edge of the continental shelf during the winter and then reverse, moving north and inshore during the summer. Most years, summer flounder show up in the northern portions of their range during May, when squid first move into the area in abundance. In the fall they have generally left their inshore waters, which are rapidly chilling, by October or early November. Most years, a cold, flooding rain usually kills off the fluke fishing in the shallow waters of my romping grounds in Connecticut and Rhode Island, by mid to late October.

From May through September fluke often move into some very shallow waters to feed, especially later in the summer when the shallow inshore beaches and bays are loaded with bait such as silversides, juvenile menhaden, anchovies, and mummichogs. Anglers generally seek fluke in waters ranging anywhere from 20 to 120 feet, with the deeper fishing being most productive early and later in the summer after inshore temperatures reach summer maximum. During the late summer, fluke can be caught in water as shallow as 5 feet when the bait is abundant.

SPAWNING

Fluke are fall spawners that drop their eggs in waters ranging from 56 to 66 degrees F during their offshore migrations, sometime between September and February, depending on which portion of the coast they are moving from.

Fluke are a fast growing, early maturing and relatively fecund fish, which accounts for their fairly rapid recovery once stringent, protective restrictions were put on both the sport and commercial fisheries during the low ebb of this species during the late 1980s and early 90s. Depending on size, fluke may mature as early as their first year, but most spawners are two and a half years of age, with males being around 10 inches and females averaging 11 to 14 inches at their first spawning.

There are two distinct spawning periods for these fish, with the largest and most intense spawn taking place during the fall, in the northern part of the range from the mid-Atlantic area north, while the southern portion of the stock drops its eggs during the late winter and early spring.

As odd looking as flounder are, being so compressed in their body form, with two eyes perched on the same side of their bodies, all species start out looking like normal fish, with one eye on each side of the body. Shortly after hatching, a juvenile flounder's eye begins migrating over to the appropriate side of its body (depending on the species and whether it's left- or right-handed) in a metamorphosis that takes 20 to 32 days (Bigelow and Shroeder), longer in cooler water temperatures.

Once both eyes are located on the same side of the head, the animal begins its life as a bottom dweller, laying on one side of its body for the rest of its life.

ADAPTATIONS AND BEHAVIORS

"Know thy quarry."

In order to be a successful angler, it is important to know the habitats in which a target species lives and how it behaves within that habitat in response to factors such as temperature, food abundance, and weather. Knowing the predatory strategies that fluke use, and what prey they prefer to feed on as the season progresses, can help catch more fish during the course of the season.

Being A Fluke

Fluke are the ultimate ambush predator, at least along the mid to north Atlantic. They remind me of the alien predator in Arnold Schwartzenegger's movie, "Predator," with the ability to disappear into the background and strike nearly unseen and at will.

Fluke aren't quite that good or high tech. However, with the ability to change color and pattern to match the bottom, and with eyes perched up like periscopes that provide excellent visibility in nearly all directions, sharp teeth, a large mouth, and good short-burst swimming ability, summer flounder are formidable predators on small fish and squid, their primary prey species. They use all of their unique adaptations to help them be the most stealthy bottom dwelling predator possible, behaving almost like a "living land mine" that explodes unseen from below, grabbing their prey before it has a chance to react.

As with all predatory species, the prey depends on the size of the predator. Small fluke eat a variety of small fish, invertebrates, worms and so forth. However, by the time fluke reach a foot in length they feed primarily on small fish, with sand eels or lancets being their primary prey and

Fluke are a top-end predator equipped with strong jaws and needle-sharp teeth, adapted for grabbing and holding squid. The jig in its mouth had a strip of squid, a soft plastic Mario's teaser and a live Arkansas shiner on the hook when this fish hit.

squid a very close second. "Find the squid and you've found the fluke," is an adage that I live by when out on the water looking for these toothy flatfish.

As with most fish, fluke are not evenly distributed throughout their habitat. Bottom structure and topography, currents, water temperature and the availability of bait are the factors that most strongly influence the whereabouts and numbers of fluke on any given day.

Until fluke migrate offshore and spawn, all they are doing during the summer months is feeding in order to grow and store as much energy as possible to get them through their spawning period and the relatively stressful and lean times of winter.

Temperature has an effect on these fish as it does with everything else that swims. One basic physical characteristic of water is the fact that the warmer it gets, the less ability it has to hold dissolved oxygen. According to a note in Bigelow and Shroeder's *Fishes of the Gulf of Maine*, fluke (and many other species) will avoid waters with dissolved oxygen levels of 3 parts per million (PPM) or below. As with many species, larger individual fluke are less temperature tolerant than juveniles and smaller individuals. During the summer smaller fluke in the 10- to 20-inch range may move into shallow warm waters to feed, while the doormats of 25 inches and up will tend to remain out in deeper, cooler waters of 60 to 100 feet or more where they feed on sand eels, squid, and other fish during the late summer heat. Again this behavior will vary with water temperatures as one travels north and south along the coast. As with all marine species fluke are most active when the tides are running. They will lay in a prime spot, which might be over or along the edge of a channel drop off, near a weed bed, beside a rock, or off a point or sand bar, and wait for the tide to deliver prey to their position. This is the reason why, once a good fluke fishing spot is located, it will probably be a good fluke spot as long as there are fish in the area, because it has the properties that this fish requires to be a successful stealth predator.

2

RODS, REELS, AND OTHER GEAR

When selecting rod and reel combos specifically for fluke fishing there are a few basic factors to consider. Fluke fishing, whether deep or shallow, is always going to be basic bottom fishing with different jig or drift rig variations. Fluke are not a species that will run much line nor pull very hard. Reels and rods can be light weight and not necessarily even of the highest or toughest quality because they will not be stressed very much by lots of fast cranking or pulling against hard-charging fish. Gear and line tests can be light and of minimal weight.

Terminal tackle should always be of minimal weight required to reach and constantly touch the bottom. The tackle should be kept light and simple. There's no need for heavy-duty reels or lines here, except for those who fish in areas of deep water and strong currents. The fact is that the weight of jigs or sinkers required to reach and hold bottom governs what style and weight of rods and line are required to effectively drift for fluke.

Even though fluking is not a terribly complex style of fishing and does not require the most finely tuned gear available, an angler who chases fluke seriously and fishes deep, shallow and in-between will need to be able to rig up two or three different line-weight rods with various actions to fish effectively under all the conditions. The more finely tuned and high quality the equipment, the easier and more enjoyable your fishing will be. Since it is necessary to be able to feel the bottom and the often light strikes from fluke, rods, reels and lines should generally be geared towards sensitivity, which means low-stretch lines, light, stiff rods, and reels with a high gear ratio and a smooth drag.

RODS

Waters ranging in depth from 50 feet up to the surf break can be fished with any light but stiff, spinning or baitcasting tackle that would be suitable for freshwater largemouth bass fishing. The specific style of rod and reel used is a matter of personal preference.

However, once depths of 50 feet or more are being probed, baitcasting tackle will do a better job at handling the heavier sinker and jig weights required to fish deeper waters. Spinning tackle that can handle six or more ounces of lead starts getting clunky and will detract from the over all sensitivity of a fishing outfit.

For handling 4- to 10-pound test Fireline, which is best for shallow water fluke fishing, a 5.5- to 7-foot medium heavy action IM-4 graphite rod, either spinning or baitcasting, is perfect.

I personally like to use spinning rods for single jig fishing techniques, and in very shallow water where some casting may be necessary. However, when drift fishing, I have a setup that my son calls "commercial trawling," which involves two identical 6-foot, medium-heavy-action bait casting rods spooled with 8-pound-test Fireline. One reel has a right hand retrieve, the other a left. This allows me to fish with two different set ups at the same time in order to determine which set up will be most effective on a given day. Once the fish are located and being caught, this "two fisted" approach doubles and even quadruples the odds of taking a fish, because there are two or even four baited hooks down below to attract a fluke.

My boat has rod holder bases spread around the entire gunnel from stem to stern, so no matter where an angler is located, there is a rod holder or two within easy reach.

When fishing with my two-rod set up, when one rod gets a hit, the other is placed in a rod holder, while the first fish is hooked and landed. While playing the first fish, it is necessary to keep an eye on the second rod in case its tip starts dancing with a second take. When double strikes occur I hand the second rod off to a partner. When alone, I feel to see which fish appears to be the largest fish and pull that one in first, leaving the second fish hooked and pulling against the drifting boat with that rod firmly secured in a Temptress lock-type rod holder.

This set up also allows me to test rigs and lures in side by side "taste tests," while fishing effectively with a known and productive rig.

For deep fluking applications in 50 to 100 feet or more of water, where large baits and heavier weights are involved, a much stouter rod is needed. An ideal light but powerful rod that can be used both for deep fluking, or trolling and eel fishing for stripers, is a heavy-action 6- or 6.5-foot "musky rod." This rod has a perfect combination of strength, power and sensitivity, in a relatively lightweight, easy to handle rod blank. Most musky rods have enough tip flex to be quite sensitive, despite their stiff lower section. It's an ideal combination for handling heavy weights in deep water.

On the other extreme, during those times when fluke are in less than 20 feet of water, heavy rigs are a hindrance. Then I use 5.5- to 6.5-foot medium-action bait or spinning rods spooled with light line and rigged with very small, light jigs, which will be described later on in this book.

REELS

To make angling as enjoyable as possible, match the size and weight of fishing reels to balance a given rod. Ideally, any rod-and-reel combination should have a balance point that is just forward of the reel or slightly towards the butt. Tip-heavy set ups become tiresome to handle and cast during a long day on the water.

For most spin fishing and bait fishing applications, size three or four reels are all that is needed. Most companies have a name and number designation on every reel that indicates its relative size. Spinning reels for fluke fishing should be 30-40, 300-400, or 3000-4000 in their size designation. For deep fluking with the musky rod, a size 4, 40, 400, or 4000 baitcasting reel is best. No particular features are required other than fast retrieve, which helps when constantly reeling rigs up from depths and keeping lines tight when fish are lunging around near the bottom. The faster one can pick up any slack line and get tight to a fighting fluke, the better the odds are that the fish will be brought to the net.

For convenience, bait casting reels that have a flipping feature are easier to use when fluke fishing, because a push of the flipping bar is all that is required to feed line back when a hit is felt or if the line pulls up off the bottom. This feature is great because it allows one-handed use when "commercial trawling" like I do, while using two reels at the same time.

Spinning reels that have bait runner features are great for many saltwater applications. By setting the tension such that the line will click if a fish takes a bait, you can "dead stick" a spinning rod while cutting bait or doing other things around the boat, particularly when action is slow. If you hear the bait runner click, reach over to the rod, reel down, and set the hook.

I also look for small, light reels that are ideal for this style of fishing and are designed for saltwater use. In the past only the big, heavy surf reels were sealed and designed to be used in saltwater. I have both Shimano Spheros, and Quantum Cabo and Boca Reels that are small, fast, and made to withstand the salt. All are excellent quality reels, but not cheap. In the long run, when purchasing fishing reels, like anything else, "you get what you pay for."

Another feature to keep in mind when choosing a spinning reel is to ensure that it has a low profile drag adjustment knob on the spool. High and straight-sided profile knobs will eventually cause trouble, because when line is reeled fast under low tension it will tend to wind around the knob, rather than the spool, causing a nasty bird's nest.

SUPER LINES

Any kind of bottom fishing and jigging can be accomplished much more effectively with a low stretch line, which in today's market means selecting some sort of a "super line" to do the job. There are many such lines available today. All have various qualities, and all feature thin diameters, little or no stretch, and high tensile strength. Some, but not all, are high performers, able to out-cast monofilaments by as much as 20 to 25 percent. Unfortunately, some are strong but too thick while others are strong, but so light and limp they constantly wrap the tip as the boat dips and rolls with the waves. Not all are made the same way and super lines are most certainly not all alike.

Some are fused and extruded fibers, others take those same fibers and braid them to make the final product. Bear in mind that braided lines such as Spider Wire (which I personally don't like) have more surface area due to the weave pattern and are usually less dense, which means more air resistance, which equates to less casting distance, and more water resistance, and hence heavier weights required to get the lure to the bottom.

Berkley Fireline is my favorite "super line" under 30 pound test for use on both spinning and bait casting rods. Fireline is made of a fused extruded "Microdynema filament, " the light, super strong material used to make flack jackets. It has a higher tensile strength than steel. When extruded into a fishing line it is very dense and slick, which means it has less water and wind resistance, so it casts farther and sinks faster than any of the braided variations or monofilaments I have used to date.

For very shallow fishing with small bait casting outfits, Whiplash 20 pound test (which is 4 pound test diameter) is a good line that allows the use of lighter weights to get deep quickly. Whiplash under 30 pound test tends to get wind knots on spinning tackle and there were rumors as of this writing that indicated it would not be produced in weights under 30 or 50 pound test, so it may not be around in the future. If this is the case, use 4, 6, or 10 pound Fireline for any and all fluke fishing applications on spinning or light bait-casting rigs to be fished in waters under 50 or 60 feet deep.

When lines must test 30 pounds or more on bait-casting rods, I prefer to use Berkley Whiplash in 100 pound test, which is the equivalent of 20 pound test monofilament or Fireline. One problem with Fireline, despite all its good qualities, is that in sizes much under 50 pound test, it will dig into the spool when a fish is caught or bottom is snagged. However, within two or three casts or drifts the line will be back to normal and performing like the world class material that it is.

Many charter captains and hard-core anglers are using Power Pro, Tuff Line and Stren's new Super Braid lines for many saltwater applications and they say they are as effective as Whiplash. I have been so satisfied with Fireline for applications under 30 pound test and Whiplash for fishing over that range that I have not seriously tested out many of the other lines on the market. Though from what I have seen, Power Pro is perhaps the best performer, though slightly behind Fireline in diameter, density and casting ability.

The point is, super lines do out-perform monofilament under most fishing conditions and they are worth the investment for a serious angler. They last much longer than mono, so over time they are actually cheaper to use. One thing that can be done with both Fireline and Whiplash, due to the fact that both are low stretch, but have no memory, when the top portion of the line becomes worn, simply reel it down on a different reel and use the other end of the line for the next couple of seasons. This will more than double or even triple the life of these super lines, making them very cost efficient in the long run.

Two tips to remember when using any super line. They don't all hold standard knots very well, so some anglers many need to learn some new knots. The Palomar, Trilene Knot, or the Double Improved Clinch Knot are three proven knots that hold up and don't slip when being used to tie slick often hard to tie super lines. My favorite is a version of the Double Improved Clinch Knot.

When tying line to lines that are of radically different diameters, or tying leaders to these super lines, use the double Uni-Knot or Uni-to-Uni knot, which is demonstrated in any good knot-tying pamphlet or in Mark Sosin's new series of knot tying videos.

By using a quality super line, matched to a sensitive rod and reel combination, the sensitivity achieved makes it possible to feel the type of bottom that is being fished and detect even the lightest strike. Knowing immediately when a fish has taken the bait is a great help in getting quick hook sets, usually making for shallow hooked fish, which should be a major concern for every conservation-minded angler. Let's face it, most of the fluke caught every summer are shorts. In order to minimize damage done to the resource in delayed hook mortality due to deep-hooking fish, anglers should design fishing methods to allow for minimal hooking damage. The best way to do that—besides using circle hooks, which I also recommend—is to feel the strike and set the hook as soon as a bite is detected, so you bring up lip-hooked fish that can be easily released with little damage.

Supersensitive rod and reel combo's also allow the angler to feel the difference in drag as soon as something is fouled up with the hooks. Any debris on a fluke rig makes it less effective. Detecting junk immediately means less down time during a drift and will increase the number of fish caught per trip. Anglers should always hold their rods so they can feel what's going on at the business end of the rig, so they can quickly clear off fouled hooks. Any of the good quality super lines will make anyone a better fluke fisherman. They all have less stretch and most are much thinner than monofilaments of the same line test. However, not all will sink faster than any equivalent monofilament or some of the competing super lines. It is necessary to experiment to find a line that best suits your personal fishing needs. Definitely rig with a top quality super line for any sort of bottom fishing, even if it is monofilament.

Since the advent of Fireline I do not use monofilament for anything, except occasionally in freshwater. Even when fishing for hard-to-hook species, a leader of fluorocarbon or green monofilament can be added for leader-sensitive species. In my experience, fluke are not line shy so when using a single jig it is tied directly to the Fireline. Flourocarbons and monofilament are used only on fluke drift rigs, which will be described later.

BOATS

Next to rod, reel, and baits, the most important piece of equipment for the fluke angler is a boat. Fluke can be caught from the shore, but having the mobility afforded by a boat, even a small one, can make a huge difference in fluke fishing success. Minimally, a 14- to 16-foot aluminum boat with high sides and a 25 to 30 hp motor is all that is needed to do some serious fluke fishing in shore and up inside coastal estuaries, river mouths and bays along most of the coast. Play the winds and tides. When conditions are flat it may be possible to get well off shore where the big fish lie. However, when seas are rough, fish in protected river or bays. Often the shallower inshore waters will produce more action than deep water areas. In close to the mainland the average fluke will be smaller, generally under three pounds, but plenty of fluke six pounds and more have been caught from less than 50 feet of water, some from bridges, jetties or even from the surf.

Electric Trolling Motors

It's important to maintain a consistent drift attitude when fluke fishing, and the best way to accomplish this goal is with an electric trolling motor. Most major manufacturers now make saltwater trolling motors that are larger and powerful enough to handle the larger boats that anglers use in the ocean, plus they are engineered and sealed for saltwater use. Bow mounted motors will pull better and make it easier to control forward movement than transom mounted motors. However when seas are rough standing in the bow can be wet and uncomfortable. The added weight up front can cause waves to slap the boat and splash inside, especially when fishing from a smaller craft. Some bow mounts themselves don't take the pounding that goes on in the ocean very well either.

However, with new generations of saltwater trolling motors on the market, odds are there is something out there that will work on any given craft. Electric trolling motors aren't critical equipment, but do make fluke fishing easier and more productive. Any serious fluke fisherman should look into purchasing one if they can afford the relatively high price tag.

Depth Finders and GPS

With so much competition for the more popular and well known fluke fishing grounds, one way to beat those crowds is to find new, more lightly fished areas and there are many throughout the region.

Obviously a depth finder is a necessary piece of equipment to locate the proper water depths, because there are times that one depth is more productive than another. In the old days, shall we say "pre GPS and Loran" days, once a productive spot was found, experienced anglers would look at the depth finder and triangulate their position from land marks, nearby pot buoys or other visible structure, then use those fixed positions to return to that same spot over and over. Effective in a general sense, but nowhere near as accurate and precise as even a cheap handheld GPS. Today all one needs to do is push a waypoint button on a GPS to enlist two orbiting satellites to put an invisible "X" on that spot.

Other Helpful Gear

A cutting board is imperative to have on a boat. Some anglers use the top of a cooler or simply lug a short wide piece of plywood or board along. Anything works but these items will bounce around while under way. All the catalogs and boating specialty shops carry some sort of removable cutting boards. Many will fit into the same locking sites as rod holders made by the same company. Most are made of Lexan or some other durable smooth surface and they work great for slicing squid or filleting on board.

Rod Holders

Rod holders are not a necessity, but it makes good sense to have a reliable rod holder of some sort available. This way an angler can place a rod into a secure holder with no chance of losing the rod over-board if a large fish hits while the rod is unattended. There are many different adjustable rod holders that also work well for trolling or simply holding rods in position while fishing. All require some sort of screwing or drilling to secure them to gunnels of most boats. Some have railing style holder mounts that are simple to install. Be sure to get a style that either offers separate holders for spinning and casting rods or some sort of clamping holder that can accommodate both types of rods.

Years ago I began using Temptress Rod Holders, which are totally adjustable with a twist lock mechanism that prevents the rod from being pulled straight out of the holder. (The real problem is not always from fish. I've had seagulls swoop down to steal a bait that is sticking up in the air and nearly pull a rod out of the boat!) A bottom snag can rip an unattended fishing rod out of the boat during a fast drift, or even shear off an inferior brand of holder, so be careful about what you buy.

Never leave anything dangling off a rod tip, either up in the air or over the side. It could catch the water and pull the rod overboard while under power. It is not a good idea to run hard with rods sticking out of rod holders like outriggers because weights and hooks can bounce around and put nicks in rod blanks that could cause sudden catastrophic breakage when put under pressure of a fighting fish or a snag. If possible, rods should be strapped in or placed in an onboard rod holder and secured for short runs over rough open water.

I have a Lund 20 Alaskan that has side storage boxes that are great for storing rods and reels while under power. I store the rods that are not in use in the large rod box by layering rigs between pieces of one-inch thick foam, cut to size to fit the box. This prevents the rods from bouncing into each other and possibly bending reel handles, bails or rod guides in rough seas. On the top of each side box I have screwed a pair of two-inch wide Velcro strips that are used to strap rods securely on this carpeted structure to keep them from falling on to the deck while under way. There are six bases to hold my six Temptress Rod Holders along each side of the boat. The result is a completely efficient system for safe rod management, using the rod holders while fishing and the Velcro straps and rod lockers providing protection while traveling from point to point.

LANDING AND FISH HANDLING EQUIPMENT

Nets are a must on any fluke trip. They should be big enough to handle the doormat of your dreams easily or a great trip can turn into a nightmare if a big fish is lost at boat side due to the lack of sufficient netting power.

Obviously, those who fish from large boats that are high off the water will require long handle nets while those fishing from lower vessels may not need a long handle, though it is a good idea to have a long handle net on board at all times in case it is needed to reach out around something to land a keeper fluke.

One friend, Mike Adams, whom I call the "Fluke Meister" because he's so skilled at catching fluke, says he always has a "personal" net on his boat for every angler, plus a net with a huge frame that he uses only for the big doormats. I have one of those nets myself, called "the wishful thinking net", because some day I hope to catch a fluke big enough to fill its huge basket. I could land a ten-year-old kid with this net, which easily handles stripers

Be sure to have a big enough net. This keeper fluke barely fits into this small net, which is ok for the little stuff but not for a ten-pound doormat. Have a "wishful thinking net" with at least a two-foot opening on hand for the fluke of a lifetime.

Bruce Guyot showing how a large net is necessary to avoid losing a doormat.

up to 30 pounds and more. Serious fluke fishermen need a net like this for that once a season situation when a big fluke is brought up to the boat. The larger net also minimizes missed fish and makes it easier for inexperienced netters to be successful when they have to use it.

Boga Grips or other caliper type, jaw-grabbing fish holders are a good tool to help control a fluke once it is landed. Boga Grips are great to hold fish for the camera and to control them for hook removal.

In addition to these caliper style grips, a small set of jaw spreaders is a helpful item to bring along on any fluke fishing trip. I have pairs on the boat and in all my tackle bags and use them when necessary to remove the hooks from any fish, toothy or smooth that have to be dehooked deep in the throat.

Spreaders are essentially a heavy wire spring that can be squeezed down, stuck sideways into closed jaws, turned upright and released to pry those jaws apart and hold them open. This allows easy access for tools such as needle nose pliers, hook removers, or surgical clamps. They come in various sizes to fit most predatory fish. They are not effective on small-mouthed fish or tiny fish but they are great for any of the larger fish that one has to handle in both fresh and saltwater. They only cost a few dollars and are a great investment for any one concerned about minimizing the damage done when removing hooks from the throats of deeply hooked and/or toothy fish.

Jaw spreaders come in sizes ranging from 4 to about 6 inches. Use the smallest set available for fluke. Even with a spreader in place, avoid placing your fingers inside a toothy mouth—if a fish flops or spins a fluke's sharp teeth can rake and cut you.

PUTTING IT ALL TOGETHER

How you rig the boat for fluking can make a big difference. Convenience is the key. Try to keep all the essentials handy either by making a specific spot for storage or adding racks and holders for various items such as nets, pliers, jaw spreaders, cutting boards and bait boxes.

Place rod holders strategically near seating positions around the boat, not just in the rear as for trolling. When fluke fishing, anglers should be encouraged to spread out to mini-mize tangles, so place rod holders where you want them to fish and on both sides of the boat so drifts can be facilitated under any wind and tide conditions.

Coolers or live wells should be placed in a central location to make it easy for all to get to them. Bait can often be split up into small personal containers with snap on caps to keep things clean and off the deck. Disposable plastic containers are ideal for bait storage in small quantities.

Nets should be placed so they can be easily reached by anyone. Whether assigned to each person or spread around in strategic locations, be sure nothing is placed on them and that the netting is not tangled in cleats or other gear. Double or triple nets on board are also a good idea when the bite is on, so everyone can land their own fish and a single net is not taken out of commission by a fish that gets fouled in the mesh with a hook or rig.

Rods not in use should be stored out of the way and out from under foot as much as possible to minimize any chance of damage.

3

FINDING THE FISH

As with most styles of fishing, being successful amounts first and foremost to locating the target species, then being able to catch them, two mutually exclusive activities, because there will be times when fish are found but for some reason they will not hit. Luckily this is the exception rather than the rule for fluke. Generally speaking, if an angler can find an area that is holding some of these toothy flatfish, they can usually be caught, unless winds and tides are working against you. Otherwise fluke will usually cooperate once bait has been presented in the proper manner—on the bottom and moving at a fair rate of drift.

Being aggressive predators, fluke will be found wherever the bait is. Their primary food is squid and fish. Squid is a favorite prey in the southern New England waters that I have fished throughout my angling career. However, fluke will also move inshore to feed on silversides, mummichogs, juvenile menhaden and other species. In the ocean fluke love squid when they are available but other species such as sand eels are a favorite and often abundant food that fluke will eat, especially in deeper waters during their migration periods.

Fluke ambush their prey from below, usually from sand or cobble bottoms. Knowing this will help the angler narrow down a search area when trying to locate fish. Watch the depth finder and wait for bottom bumps to flatten out. Fluke may be found along channel edges or in breaks in eelgrass and other vegetation, but they will not suspend over the weeds or sit in them to hunt their prey. The exception to this rule is when there is a definite flow of water carrying bait over holes and pockets that will provide fluke a holding spot and easy access to prey. In nature, nothing is ever true all the time. Once while spearing blackfish I saw a fluke draped over a rock a few feet above the sand bottom. That fluke was so big I didn't realize it was a fish until it disappeared in a flip of its tail. During the late summer, when shallow inshore bays and inlets are full of small fish, fluke will move into some very skinny water and for a long ways up into tide creeks to pursue bait. They will lay off the mouths of smaller tide creeks and along the edge of eelgrass flats, to ambush fish that are pulled out of these areas by dropping tides. This is a more common behavior in the south, where tide flats are more extensive, than in New England.

LOOKING SHALLOW

The oddest fluke catch I ever made was at Hilton Head, South Carolina.

I am not a golfer but was down at Hilton Head working on a dolphin study with a dozen science teachers from our school district. A cabbie had told me that the saltwater ponds around the development had some fish, mostly tarpon, weakfish, and drum that would come in through feeder pipes as juveniles, and become trapped. They never grew to their full potential in these micro-habitats, but there were some decent sized fish in these small, protected salt ponds. They could be fished from the access road without upsetting the residents who owned mansions along the water's edge, as long as I stayed along the roadside of these waters.

At the first opportunity, I rode a rental bike along the access road, stopping and fishing any fishable water that was near the pavement. I had a light two-piece spinning rod and a pocket full of Slug Go's, twister tails, swimming plugs and small jigs—an array of lures designed to catch freshwater bass and perhaps a drum or weakfish.

One such pond was fed by an upright pipe with water bubbling in from the incoming tide. I saw a small tarpon jump as I approached so I stopped to take a few casts. Before long a guy pulled off the road in his truck and began to rig up for some fishing. He had a pail of live killifish and a light spinning rod. He hooked up a bait, added a bobber about three feet above the hook, and lobbed it underhand, about ten feet from the bank into a small channel of moving water caused by the flood from the pipe.

He sat down on a second pail and we began to talk fishing.

Almost instantly, his bobber began to dip, move, and slowly sunk out of sight. He reared back and set the hook on what I hoped would be a drum or tarpon, being I had never seen either species in the flesh. A couple of heave hauls, some wild reel cranking and he had a three-pound fluke flopping in the manicured grass on the bank beside the pond.

He evidently saw the envy on my face and offered me a live bait, which I immediately scarfed up. I offered him a fluke for minnow exchange program, which he happily accepted as we chuckled over the trade agreement.

I took a small jig head, stuck it up through the lips of a minnow and tossed it out into the now fading current and began to work it slowly along the bottom in what was about three or four feet of water.

I used two minnows, in two casts, which yielded fluke of 3.5 and 4.5 pounds, while he landed another couple of fish before the tide ran out. His five-gallon pail was looking like a bouquet of fluke tails flapping in the breeze as the tide hit high slack and the bite abruptly ended.

I had to be back for a meeting and left that interesting spot without getting another shot at either the fluke or tarpon.

I couldn't believe it, fluke in what looked like a little salty "water hole." Very interesting, but an insight as to the fact that

Fluke from the South Carolina salt pond that was full of fluke like the 3-pounders I'm holding. These fish like it shallow.

fluke will move up into some very skinny water, when water temperature and oxygen levels are right, provided that a source of food is also present.

In southern New England where I have done most of my fluking, fluke come in close to shore and well up inside rivers late in the summer and early fall, when small bait is most abundant in the shallows. Most of the doormats will remain in deeper waters, but the small stuff with some "Joey's" (the commercial term for jumbo, four-pound-plus fluke) mixed in will move miles up large rivers and cruise the surf break, feeding on peanut bunker. Every summer, as I call various tackle shops throughout the region for information to write weekly columns, there is a time, usually later in August, when the fluke catch suddenly drops off.

It is true that by late summer with constant pressure from both recreational and commercial fishermen, fluke populations become "picked over" and reduced in some areas. But there are many places holding fluke that get little or no pressure at all! Some are small coves, minor drop offs, zones between the popular places that guys like me constantly write about that will hold good numbers of fish and few anglers. Locating some of these places is one way to get your "body count" back up to par. It takes some experimentation and searching for such places, but when you find them the fishing can often be quite good.

Years ago, when mortgages were new and the kids small, I didn't have the money to buy and maintain much of a boat. The best I could do at that time was a very seaworthy 14-foot Lund aluminum, a very well built, solid boat that takes the water like a champ.

With my small boat I was the first to duck for cover when things kicked up. Wind and bad weather forced me to find protected inshore spots—and I mean "spots," some not much larger than my boat—in the areas I fished. By being off the beaten path, trolling with an electric motor in places that few if any other fluke fishermen ever hit, my efforts paid off.

One day my wife and I caught and released something like 38 fluke up to 6 pounds, during a half a tide in the Mystic River. There were no limits in those days but I never kept all the fish I caught and had a personal boat limit of 16 inches, long before it was the law of the seas. We did not usually have any trouble sticking with our self imposed larger size limits, even during the days when fluke populations were at their all time low in 1989 and 1990.

We caught those fish by spotting dark shadows made by schools of baby bunker that were cruising around in a shallow area that was between 6 and 12 feet deep. Every time we found the schools and drifted through them we whacked a couple of fluke. It was a lesson that has stuck with me ever since.When the bite slows in the usual 40 to 50 foot depths, try running up into shallow water and locating some bait, because that's what the fluke have done. They have moved inshore to take advantage of that abundant food source.

With this in mind, numerous times over the past twenty seasons, I have used this little trick to salvage what have some times been awful outings in the deep-water fluking grounds. But it only works later in the summer when inshore temps are in the 70's and there are loads of small fish along the beaches and in the bays to draw them in to shallow waters.

This skinny-water fishing trick was a scenario that I drew upon once again just last summer.

I took a friend out to sample what we had both heard was a great "big fluke" bite along the south shore of Fishers Island.This particular day, the fish were there but the weather wasn't.

Winds kicked up against the tides, and even changed when the tide did, so we couldn't ever get a good drift with the winds and tides running in the same direction. Not wanting to waste any more of our time, we decided to end the trip. On our way in to the launch, there was a barrier island with the main channel curving around its west end, where it carved a 30-foot hole that often holds a few fish.

It was and still is a busy channel, so most of the time it was impossible to drop a line in without getting in someone's way, but we decided to give it a try, being that the flooding tide and wind were aligned in this particular spot.

I planned to drift along the edge of this hole out of the traffic, hoping there would be some fluke down there to catch.We set the lines in about 30 feet of water, watching the depth finder as we drifted up out of that hole at a 45-degree angle into about 12 feet of water around its rim. Neither of us had so much as a single "tap-tap" in the depths where we expected to find fish. However, as the boat reached the top edge of the hole and began drifting out over a flat that ran a couple hundred yards in towards shore, I got a whack from a keeper fluke in about 9 feet of water.

My partner laid his rod down to net my fish and had a clone on his line when he picked it back up. Initially he thought that he was snagged in the eelgrass, because the boat was only in five feet of water. By now, the tide was sweeping powerfully up over this flat, which has a sandy bottom with patches of eel grass, punctuated with plenty of holes, pockets and pathways between these clumps to hide a hungry shallow-feeding fluke.

We ran back to the edge of the hole and repeated the drift a couple of dozen times. In the process, we culled out the rest of our two-man limit of fish ranging from just keepers, which was 16 inches at that time, to about 18 inches. Nothing to brag about, but good-sized fish that saved that particular trip.

The fun part was we caught that limit in clear shallow water and actually saw many of the fluke take the small baited ¼-ounce jigs we were drifting with in that very shallow water. The fish are so well camouflaged that even in clear water the waves hid the shape of most of the fish we caught. Our little white squid jigs would simply disappear before our eyes; we'd set the hook and lift the fish into the boat, cane pole style.

It was fun, a trip saver and a lesson to remember, because there are many places like this one described along the fluke coast.

FISH CHANNELS

Most shallow water fluke fishing, in water less than 40 feet deep, will be inshore—either along beaches or around river mouths. In these areas always look for fluke just over and along the edge of any sort of drop off as you move out from the beach searching for fish. Often the contours along beaches will drop off in terraces that have been carved out of the bottom by moving tides. The water depth will be level, and then it drops off a few feet, levels off again, and so forth. Fluke will concentrate just over the top and near the bottom of those drop offs.

In close to shore, look for fluke to concentrate in the drop offs into natural or dug channels. Whether they are small, shallow channels that run through a shallow flats area, or a deep shipping channel, all are likely to hold fish at some time during the season. Most river channels, or the channels dug into the bottom outside a salt pond, for instance, will hold fluke all season long.

When tides drop bait is flushed out of river shallows adjacent to channels, so the fluke (and other predatory species) will wait in ambush as the bait is drawn from the relative safety of the shallows, into the open, deeper waters of the channel. Often they will lie on the "down tide edge" of a channel or near the rim of the channel edge, when the high tide is pushing bait in towards the shallows and shore.

Watch your depth finder constantly and pay attention to slight differences in depth, and work these places hard. Fluke will very often lie just over the lip of a channel edge, especially if it is a slight difference in depth of say two to four feet. Channels are natural funnels and should never be overlooked whether they are 5, 20 or 125 feet deep. In larger coastal rivers, such as the Thames and Housatonic Rivers in my home state of Connecticut, fluke will follow baby menhaden up these large channels and feed their way, often for miles, upstream during the late summer and fall.

DEEPER EDGES AND DROP OFFS

Fluke fishing in shallow water is always easier because it requires less weight to reach and hold bottom. Unfortunately shallow water fluking does not work all of the time. Over the long haul, the best fluke fishing will be found along deeper stretches of the coast, wherever the tides sweep through, carrying a bounty of baitfish and squid. Find the squid and you've found the fluke.

When fishing in a new area, always keep a topo map handy and use the depth finder to locate drop offs and edges where ever they may occur. A classic example of ideal fluke habitat can be found along the south shore beaches of Rhode Island, or along the perimeter of Long Island or Montauk Point, where some of the best fluke fishing in the region can be experienced.

Typically, when fishing out off the Rhode Island beaches, there are a couple of terrace-like drop offs, the first at the surf break where waters slope gently out to 30 to 40 feet, then there is a quick drop to 50 or 60 feet and a gradual taper out into deeper waters a mile or more off the mainland.

The edges of these drop offs are not necessarily straight. In fact, they are anything but straight, with points and sunken peninsulas creating excellent fluke fishing structure. The contours here often trace a wavy line along the entire beach, a line that constantly shifts with the tides and major storms, which can move tons of sand around on the bottom. Major storms can totally change the make up of a given spot, sometimes literally over night.

For years, there was a great little drop off, which I called "the trough," which was more like a shallow gulch that slanted out away from the beach at a gradual angle that took the bottom depth from 15 to 45 feet.

I had fished this little trench for ten years and it always seemed to hold fish. It was my "go to" spot when I was looking for a quick fluke for supper or to impress a guest with a good catch of fish.

The year of the "Perfect Storm," the coast was battered by a series of hard nor'easters. The storm that sank the Andrea Gale hit the New England coast and blew hard for days.

The following season I took a friend to my little "fluke hole" and it was gone! I mean gone, filled in by the erosion from the series of powerful storms the previous fall that had pulled tons of sand off the beaches and deposited it in my little trough. Where it had been 35 to 36 feet, it was all the same 26 to 28 foot depths, no drop offs to fish and consequently no more fluke honey hole.

By the end of that summer and the following summer it had dug itself back out again, but the deepest part of the trench was only about 31 or 32 feet, enough to once again consistently hold fluke most of the time.

When fishing shallow waters you'll find that most of the fluke fishing fleet is out in 50 to 80 feet of water fishing heavier weights and dealing with deeper water. We are in 30 feet, using lighter tackle, feeling the bites better and usually catching just as many often more fluke, though perhaps with not quite as many fish over 6 pounds as the guys drifting in the deeper waters out to 100 feet.

One reason I don't like fishing out in those more open waters is because the draggers hit it hard often under the cover of darkness. When they are working and their quota is open, fishing with rod and reel becomes a lot more difficult. One never knows if a dragger has recently vacuumed the bottom clean. By working the inshore drifts, where depths vary, ledges may protect certain stretches of water from the deadly trawlers. I like to fish in areas that have lots of lobster pots. Though the pots themselves can pose a problem when drifting, with ghost pot trawls often eating up gear, at least you can be assured that no one has run a net through areas where pots are close together. When fishing along beaches and their drop offs, try to find a sunken point to drift along, over, or around. Odds are your catch will be improved. These areas of underwater structure, no matter how large or small, will often be fluke magnets. Some are large enough to locate on a map, others you will have to find for yourself, by paying attention when fluke are hooked and noting if it appears to be near some sort of hole, rise, or drop off. Marking waypoints on a GPS is the simplest way to put an "X" on a given spot.

Fish will generally be on the down-tide side of such bottom structure. There will usually be a band of water of a certain depth where most of the fish appear to be holding at a given point in any tide. Once that depth is located, limiting out is a snap.

At times when the fluke may be in deeper areas without much in the way of drop offs or other structure, depth bands are the only thing to go by. When searching out new places in deeper water (or shallow water for that matter), look for slick lines, tide lines, anything that may give away a tide shear, or any place where the currents or wind drifts are different. They are all over the place out in the ocean, often holding debris on the surface that floats above something that will hold fish below the surface. "When in doubt, fish a slick line."

Fish near—to but not too close—to pot buoys. Lobster pots are essentially a chum pot that often holds fluke nearby, but you have to avoid hooking into their lines.

FISH THE LOBSTER POTS

One day, when I first started seriously targeting fluke, I learned "the lesson of the lobster pots."

We had been fishing a channel, primarily down the center in its deepest part, and were picking up a few fish, but working much too hard for each bite.

At one point I noticed that the few fish we were catching were near the end of each drift and just down tide from a cluster of about three lobster pots. Earlier that day I had seen the owner of these pots check and replace the bait. Thinking that perhaps the bait in the pots was acting like chum, we narrowed our drift to less than 50 yards down current from this spot and began to pick up fish at a greatly increased rate.

Noting this pattern the boat was run in closer to shore and maneuvered through a maze of pots. We hammered the fish for the remainder of the tide and were culling for doormats within an hour. Our best fluke that day was around six pounds.

Lobster pots generally do two things for the wary fluke fisherman. First, they are usually set on, around, or near some sort of hard structure or drop offs, at least in the shallower inshore areas of southern New England. This gives anglers an edge along which to drift, an edge that is likely to hold and concentrate fluke.

One problem with fishing near shoreline structure at the present time, when porgy populations are at very high levels, is "the porgy factor. " These abundant and aggressive little fish will often chew up and steal fluke baits long before the fluke have a chance to grab hold. For this reason I always fish with a scented plastic Mario's Squid Strip on jigs also baited with natural bait. If the scup, crabs, or cunners steal the real baits, the plastic, especially scented plastic strips, usually survives and will continue to attract attention and draw strikes from fluke even without live or cut bait.

WATCH THE THERMOMETER

Fluke are a warm water species that likes water temperatures up into the high 60s and 70s. Temperature becomes a factor most often early and late in the season, as fluke are moving in or off shore, and at the northern extreme of their range, where temperatures are cooler.

Fluke arrive first in our area during May in the Point Judith, Rhode Island area, when surface water temps are still in the 50s. Fluke show up when squid move in from off shore and remain in the region as long as temperatures stay within their comfort zone, but dropping temperatures and dwindling daylight cause them to leave their shallow inshore haunts abruptly every fall.

Often there will be a cold, rainy few days in October that turns the inshore fluking off like a faucet along the Connecticut coast. We can be catching large numbers of fluke, mostly small stuff feeding underneath swarms of peanut bunker on Sunday, have heavy rains and chilly nights drop the temperatures of the river back into the high 50s, and by Tuesday all those fluke were gone, probably to their fall staging areas in various locations along the coast.

In our area Block Island, the south side of Fishers Island, Gardners Island and Montauk Point are areas where fluke that are migrating off shore seem to concentrate and "stage" before moving off shore each fall.

Along most of the southern New England coast, fluke will be found along the beaches, up into bays and rivers where water temperatures will range into the mid to high 70 degree F range.

However, in the northern extent of the fluke's range, at least the range where anglers bother to target them, is Cape Cod.

The Cape is a notoriously fertile fluke fishing area among aficionados, though it is far better known for its striper, tuna and cod fishing. My friend Mario Tirone and a number of other hard core "fluke meisters" from as far away as Delaware and Pennsylvania make annual migrations to the Cape.

There is a notable contrast when fishing the much cooler waters of the Cape as compared to fishing warmer waters of Long Island or Block Island Sounds.

My wife Karen holds up a 4-pound fluke that's being inspected by Mario Tirone's dog Samantha. The fish was caught in the fall off Provincetown on Cape Cod. The Cape has some great fluke fishing, though most fishermen think of striped bass, tuna and cod when traveling there.

During the latter part of warm summers, fluke may be driven off into deeper, cooler waters by warm surface and inshore temperatures in Long Island Sound, the opposite situation occurs in the cold, fringe waters of the Cape.

When fishing the Cape Cod during the summer months, rather than worry about whether the fluke are in 50, 60, or more feet of water, all anglers need to do is fish out from shore along what would be the shallow, first drop off, usually in less that 40 or 50 feet of water. The deeper waters, which will run in the 50s, are cooler than the fluke like, preferring the warmer water inside bays, shallow coves and pockets such as the protected part of Cape Cod Bay inside the hook at Provincetown.

I've fished Provincetown on a number of occasions with Mario Tirone and we always seek out waters that are less than

50 feet and with the highest water temperatures we can find. Naturally, because of the cooler water, things will shut down earlier and more abruptly in the fall. However, while the fishing holds up, this popular tourist destination is also one of the best, uncrowded fluke fishing regions of the coast.

4

JIGS, RIGS, AND STRATEGIES FOR CATCHING FLUKE

Unlike many other sport fish, which will move up and down through the water column in response to light intensity, temperature and food availability, fluke are bottom dwellers and therefore must always be targeted right on the bottom.

Occasionally, summer flounder, which are very aggressive predators, will chase bait up to the surface. Surf fishermen sometimes see fluke chasing bait in the face of breaking waves, just like striped bass or blues. One fluke specialist I know told me that on more than one occasion he has seen fluke pushing bait to the surface in 120 feet of water! But such events are rare, so concentrate your fishing within a few inches of terra firma.

Fishing and rigging for fluke is relatively simple and can be broken down into three general classes: drift baits, drift rigs (which use jigs rather than sinkers to reach bottom), and jigs. Rarely there may be a fourth class, free swimming live baits that would be employed in shallow waters. There are situations when simply fishing with an unweighted live baitfish, such as a mummichog, will work on fluke, using floats (bobbers) to keep baits just above the bottom. Such situations will be rare in the northeast, but more common in the south, where anglers fish in extensive areas of shallow flats and tidal rivers and creeks.

DRIFT BAITS

Many anglers caught their first fluke on a "fluke drift rig" that can be purchased in any tackle shop. It consists of a sinker off a three way swivel, with about three feet of heavy monofilament back to a series of attractor spinners and beads strung ahead of a large, size 2/0 to 4/0 hook, that may have hair, a plastic skirt, or teaser added to attract bites.

Strips of bait, squid, fish, or a combination of the two are placed on the hook. The sinker is lowered to the bottom and dragged with the prevailing winds and tide, often on a much too heavy boat rod, with twice as much lead in the sinker as is needed to reach and hold bottom.

These bait rigs were the standard fluke rig three to four decades ago and they are still available and popular today because they continue to catch fluke. It is the rig that I caught my first fluke on. However since that time, I have found some lighter and more fun to fish rigging methods that will be discussed later in this chapter.

Drift rigs are the most effective rigs for dragging fluke off the bottom in deep waters of 80 feet or more, especially when

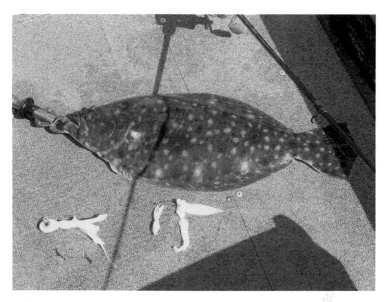

A drift rig, consisting of a jig to a three-way swivel and five feet back to a dropper hook, which has a Luhr Jensen B-2 squid with a bead ahead of the hook, and baited with a strip of real squid and a live Arkansas shiner. The shiner was lost on the way to the net.

the tide is running hard or under windy conditions. By varying the sinker size, and attaching them with a snap swivel or loop, this rig can be quickly adapted to changing wind and current conditions between drifts. In deep water, holding bottom may require 6, 8 or more ounces of lead, especially when fishing with large baits that have more surface area and therefore drag. Deep water is where that heavy rod is most practical. A stiff, heavy rod is necessary to handle the heavy sinker weights required to reach and hold bottom efficiently in deep water. But keep the rod as light and sensitive as possible to add fun and help in detecting the often light take of even a large fluke.

This style of deep fluking is not as much fun as using light tackle in the shallows, but it is an effective method for reaching and catching those huge doormats, that often hold in deeper, cooler, tide-swept waters during the heat of the summer.

Drift rigs can be modified for use with light tackle, by reducing the size of the sinker for shallower applications. When in shallower waters even the hook and spinner blades can be scaled down to accommodate lighter rods and lines.

A variation on drift rig fishing comes from freshwater large-mouth bass fishing. For years largemouth bass anglers have used soft plastic lures on a Carolina Rig, which is essentially a slip sinker or weight a short distance from the hook and lure. Cat fishermen employ a similar set up, which allows the hook to slip without any detectable drag through a slip sinker when a catfish strikes.

Fluke fishermen fishing from a boat in shallow water or from shore rig up a slip sinker above a barrel swivel, which is tied with a leader to a baited hook. The bait could be a single live minnow or a minnow-squid combo. This allows the angler to cast and slowly retrieve this rig. When a fluke strikes line is paid out for a short time before setting the hook.

The classic fluke drift rig can be used effectively in any depth of water from the surf break to over 100 feet where the doormats lie.

FREE LINING AND FLOATS

Free lining baits or fishing off floats are the way to go when fluke are concentrated in very shallow water. Small jigs also do the trick in less than 10 feet of water. Live bait drifted off a float or swimming free in the shallows is perhaps the ultimate attractant, when it comes to drawing strikes from fluke, or any other predator for that matter.

Floats are most useful from shore when employed to drift baits, using winds or currents, out to places where the fish may be holding, which may be well beyond casting range. The problem is, when drifting baits for fluke that must be on or very near the bottom to be effective, drifting a bait out with the tide will only work if the water is shallow and uniform in depth for a long distance off the shore. Otherwise if the bottom drops off into deeper water, a bobber will hold the bait only a few feet from the surface and will more likely draw strikes from striped bass or bluefish. Boat fishermen under the same conditions would vertically jig, while drifting over the fishing grounds with the prevailing winds and tides.

I've seen fishermen successfully catch fluke by drifting baits with floats or balloons along jetties and piers where bottom depths are consistent. Late in the summer, when fluke push peanut bunker up into shallow bays, inlets and river mouths, this method works well because it keeps hook baits just above the bottom where they are less likely to snag.

This method will only work under very specific conditions that are most common in the mid and southern Atlantic areas, and very seldom appropriate for southern New England waters.

JIGS

Over the past 30 years, most of the serious fluke fishermen I know have exchanged their sinker drift rigs for jigs rigged in various combinations including single, tandem, or jig and dropper combinations, all of which work very well under a wide variety of conditions, in waters anywhere up to 60 or 70 feet. Over 70 or 80 feet, especially when the tide is running hard, most jigs are too light to reach and hold bottom. At this point it is time to change over to a classic drift rig, so enough weight can be added to drag bottom throughout the entire drift.

Fishermen to the south in Delaware and Chesapeake Bay have been jigging fluke for years and their technique finally migrated north with the fluke and those who chase them about 25 or 30 years ago.

I was introduced to this highly productive technique like a slap in the face one hot summer day over 25 years ago by a college student "J-R" Roy, who was working for me as a seasonal assistant in the 1970's, back when I was in charge of the Marine Recreational Fisheries Program for the Connecticut DEP.

"J.R." was born and raised in Mystic, so he knew the Mystic River and near by waters very well. On top of that, he worked weekends on a charter boat that fished out of Block Island. The charter mostly chased stripers and tuna, but occasionally they did some fluke fishing around the perimeter of these excellent fluking grounds.

Fluke Fishing Epiphany #1

J.R. and I and a mutual friend took a busman's holiday from our fisheries work with the DEP to go fluking. It was mid-July and these toothy critters were cruising the Connecticut coast in abundance. The other guy and I brought our classic sinker-style drift rigs, complete with beads and spinners, baited with squid strips, while J.R. broke out his jigs, which were also tipped with strips of squid.

J.R. immediately began hooking up. Five fish later, to our combined zero hits, and after some serious taunting, he offered us a couple of his jigs to try. We both immediately snatched them up and started catching fluke right along with him. I've been jigging fluke one way or another ever since.

That day, rather than fishing with the heavy, insensitive level wind boat rod I was using with those heavy drift rigs, I tied my jig to a light spinning rod. It was an eye opener for me.

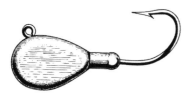

The flat head jig overcomes upswell currents and the thin, flat shape allows lighter weights to reach deeper.

Any type of stand-up jig is effective for fluke.

Sparkie jig, whose forward-balance design pulls over snags and also rests flat on the bottom, which allows it to be used with a sliding action.

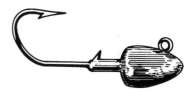

Arrowhead jig, whose flat, tapered shape gets through strong currents and gives more side-to-side action to whatever is on the body or the hook.

Banana or boxing-glove style. One of my favorite fluke jigs in shallow water because it skims over debris and weeds better than some other designs.

Spearhead jig, one of many bullet-type jigs that work well in deep water and fast currents.

A variety of jig-head styles that I like to use for fluke. (Courtesy Do-It Corporation, *www.do-itmolds.com*)

That day, on my light spinning rod, working a half-ounce bucktail baited with a couple of strips of squid, I discovered the joys and challenges of fluke fishing. With a light, sensitive freshwater bass rod in hand working a jig was not only much more fun than dragging three or four ounces of lead like an anchor along the bottom, it was also a heck of a lot more effective.

By switching over to light tackle and jigs, my fluke catch average immediately increased by four or five fold.

With the light but stiff spinning rod, strikes could be felt much more readily, so hooking fish was much easier. The fluke we hooked, especially those weighing over three pounds, put up a decent fight, which made them a great deal more enjoyable to catch. One of the larger fish I caught that day, a four and a half pounder, actually took a couple of feet of line against the drag and made a pretty good account of itself. We each caught over a dozen nice fluke up to about 4 or 5 pounds, good action, great fun and terrific table fare.

In those days, there were no size or catch limits, though we always had a personal minimum length of 16 or 17 inches. Besides, none of us could stand to clean more than six or eight fish at a time, so even though we often caught large numbers of fluke, we never "filled the freezer" just because we could. I've always fished by the credo: "Take only what you need, not all you can catch."

Over the next few years I realized how challenging and enjoyable fluke were to catch and began logging progressively more time targeting these interesting and challenging bottom dwellers. Fluke are much more of a finesse fish than the harder fighting stripers, bluefish, sharks and tuna that had dominated my marine fishing interests to that point.

Over the years I began tailoring and customizing both spinning and light bait casting tackle and rigs to make fluke fishing not only more enjoyable, but much more effective. By switching from light spinning rods, with small (less than half ounce) jigs for the shallows, to medium action six foot freshwater bass tackle (bait casting or spinning) for medium depth fishing, then to heavier bait casting tackle for the deep water heavy weight fishing, it was possible to maximize catches and target fluke of all sizes throughout the season with great success.

Along with designing matched rods and reels that maximized the efficiency and enjoyment of fluking, I also began playing around with various rigging techniques to see what worked the best.

In those days, my kids were young and frequently along on my inshore trips. The kids would use what ever happened to be the hottest fluke rig at the time, while I would fish two identical rods, one with a right hand reel, and the other with a left.

Dirt simple, a jig baited with a strip of squid and a mummichog is one of the best shallow-water fluke rigs anywhere.

One would be rigged out with the same thing as the kids; the other would have some variation or a completely new experimental rig.

I call it "side by side taste testing, " which helped evolve the rigging styles that are employed very effectively at the present time. Though the "taste testing" is constantly going on to try out new drift rigs, teasers, and baits, a basic drift rig using a jig with a non-weighted dropper is my current go-to set up and has been for over 20 years.

To sweeten the offerings, add a live mummichog, fresh or frozen silversides, or sand eel on top of the fresh squid strip to add flash, movement (in live baits) and smell. A jig with a live fish of some sort will usually out-fish a jig with just a strip of cut frozen or fresh squid.

One day I was complaining to Joe Balint, who runs the Fish Connection about having my mummy pot stolen and no fresh live baits on the previous trip. Joe suggested some freshwater shiners (Arkansas shiners) that most shops sell for freshwater fishing. He'd been using the dead ones from the tanks in his shop for his own fluke fishing and said that they worked as well as any frozen fish bait and that the live ones worked even better.

Even though they are a freshwater species, Arkansas shiners, if kept in a large bait bucket with oxygen tabs or an aerator, will survive a day of fishing. On the hook, they live more than long enough to draw the attention of any fluke that's on the prowl. If they die, they hold on the hook better than frozen fish of any kind. Plus they have more flash and wiggle than any dead or frozen bait. Though more expensive than catching your own bait, if time is of the essence, as it usually is with me, buying a couple of dozen fresh shiners for a fluke fishing trip (if live mummies couldn't be caught or purchased) is a better alternative than any frozen fish bait.

Plastic teasers vary in style, size and color, ranging from molded life-like squids (my personal favorite), to plastic offshore teaser skirts, plastic squid strips, and curley tails. All work—it's a matter of tailoring them to the lure and conditions.

The final evolution to developing the ultimate jig for fluke fishing was the addition of a soft plastic teaser to the jig. Any sort of white chartreuse or pink twister tail, worm or other small piece of soft plastic will do. However, for the average ⅝ to ounce or heavier jigs used for mid range fluking, a 4-inch scented Mario's Soft Plastic Squid Strip is the "Ultimate Teaser, " as it says on the package.

The basic procedure is to take a jig that is just heavy enough to reach and skim bottom, add a soft plastic teaser, on top of that add a strip or two of cut frozen squid, a strip of fluke or sand dab belly meat, and top the whole mess off with a fish of some sort, live if possible—the bigger the fish the better. Jumbo, four inch long striped killifish or a snapper bluefish, are the best live baits for big fluke. However, even the wiggle of a small living mummichog or Arkansas shiner adds enough "life" to this rig to tempt even a large doormat. I once caught a 7.75-pound doormat on the last mummichog of the day, a tiny little one that was barely an inch and a half long. So even though big bait usually means big fish, a wiggle from a little live bait should not be ignored.

I call the jig, soft plastic teaser, with a real squid strip and fish bait added on top, a "fluke sandwich. " It is a rigging style that is considered by many to be "the" classic jig fishing method for fluke in my area.

This fluke hit a swimming jig called a Salt Shaker, by Lunker City, one of my favorite schoolie striper lures, as it was ripped over a shoal point in the Mystic River in three feet of water.

Depending on the size of the jig being used, the plastic teasers and fish can be tailored to fit the rigging.

For instance, in very shallow water or on a slow drift, where a ¼- to ½-ounce jig is all that's required to hit and bounce bottom, go with a small white, chartreuse or pink auger tail soft plastic teaser or even a half of a white plastic worm that is split down the middle. Add a 3 to 4-inch piece of squid and a small bait fish. For very shallow fluke fishing, less than 20 feet, my personal favorite jig is a Luhr Jensen B-2 squid jig in day glow color, baited as noted above with squid and fish.

Standard jigs of a half ounce and heavier, can handle a 4-inch Mario's Squid Strip, one or two 4- to 6-inch strips of real squid, and a larger minnow or mummichog. The fluke will eat it like candy.

In deep waters, where a 2 to 3 ounce or larger jig is required, switch to a 6-inch soft plastic Mario's Squid Strip, a whole small squid, fillet of hickory shad or other large bait. Otherwise use the largest strips of squid that can be made from the available bait, topped with the largest fish possible.

When fluke rigs become large, in excess of 6 inches, with the primary bait a shad fillet, whole squid or maybe a whole herring or tinker mackerel, it is a good idea to add a stinger hook to the terminal end of the entire bait rig. As a rule of thumb, I tie a hook that is roughly half the size of the hook on the jig to the eye of the jig or to the shank of the hook, with 16 or 20 pound test and stick it in the furthest end of the bait. This technique will minimize having the bait nipped off just behind the hook. A stinger hook will eliminate this aggravation and increase your catch by 30 to 50 percent.

A few years ago, when size limits increased to 17 or 18 inches, I stopped using stingers, except when fishing deep for jumbo fish with huge baits, because the small hook will increase the number of deep hooked fish caught. Unfortunately under current regulations, which will probably be with us for ever, most of the increase in catch from the stinger hook will be shorts, so its probably better if they are not caught to begin with. Still, a stinger hook is a great way to be sure that a high percentage of fish that hit are hooked on those days when fishing is slow.

Be aware that by adding all this extra stuff, especially the soft plastics, some of which float, will add buoyancy to the overall rig. This circumstance will sometimes require going to a slightly heavier jig to compensate. The trade off in increased catch is well worth coping with the additional weight.

All of the "junk on the hook," especially the soft plastic, will make the jig plane, slide and glide in the water with a more squid-like motion. A simple baited lead head and hair jig, which is "lead heavy, " bounces unnaturally, like a yo-yo. It does not have the natural, sliding action of a "fluke sandwich," which glides and slides with the hook held out and slightly elevated, making it easier for a fish to take the hook into its mouth. Since fluke conform to the adage that "big baits mean big fish," adding multiple offerings to the hook will not deter fish from striking. In fact, the larger profile is more likely to attract the attention of a large "Joey" (the commercial term for jumbo) or "doormat" fluke.

A second, very important factor in adding a soft plastic teaser is that it becomes a fallback system to keep the lure fishing effectively should the natural bait be stolen or drop off. When drifts are slow and crabs or skate get hold of baits, or later in the summer when the "porgy factor" comes into effect, a soft plastic teaser can save the day. Scup are bait stealers of the first order. When I first met Mario Tirone, the guy who invented and began making Mario's Plastic Squid Strips in his basement, he would fish with nothing but a jig and one of his creations, simply to prove to me that it worked. Since then he often fishes only with the plastic teaser because it is simpler and cleaner than handling stinky, slippery baits. Mario catches loads of fluke every year on nothing but a jig and one of his "ultimate teasers," a scented plastic Mario's Squid Strip, which also works very well for striped bass and off shore for shark and tuna.

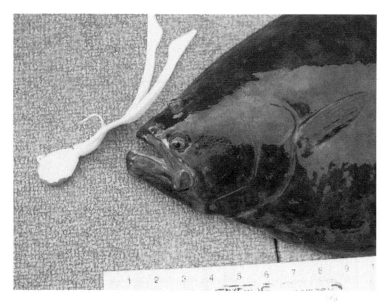

Fluke with a jig with Mario's Plastic Squid Strip Teaser. Top this with a strip of squid and a large live fish of some sort and you have the basic fluke rig for medium to larger fish.

Granted, fishing with just a bare jig and soft plastic tail is not as effective as fishing with a baited "fluke sandwich," but it will catch enough fluke, to make it worth while should the need arise, on a whim or under a "salvage the trip" situation.

DIFFERENT JIGS FOR DIFFERENT RIGS

There are nearly as many styles of jig heads as there are methods of rigging for fluke. Each design variation has a specific objective in mind when it comes to running style, how rapidly it sinks, skims or holds bottom.

The first jig styles I used years ago were bullet jigs and small "Smiling Bills" which are what the "Do It" jig molding catalog calls a "Hot Lips" Jig. They can be molded in sizes up to 5 ounces so will fill many of the needs of fluke fishermen who ply the deepest waters of 100 feet or more under most conditions. Designed more for trolling and jigging striped bass, I only use the largest models for deep-water forays, because that "smile" will scoop up more bottom debris when dragging bottom, than a more tapered design.

Another good, deep water jig head, designed to sink fast and get down deep with less weight, is a "Flathead Jig" that can be poured on your own or purchased in sizes up to 4 ounces. Mario Tirone markets these jig heads for striped bass, but I use them for fluke in deep waters with a 7-inch Squid Strip for the doormats.

Many freshwater jig heads are made with "Round Head" jigs, which for some reason are not employed as much with a molded hook for fluke. However, there is a "Round Ball" style fluke jig with a free-swinging hook that may or may not have hair or Mylar tied to it as a teaser. The most popular styles are chromed with a fly-like hook that is baited "fluke sandwich" style and fished very effectively in deeper waters because it comes in sizes up to 8 ounces. Unfortunately the single hooks on the large ball jigs are small, so I will occasionally tie on a second tandem hook when fishing them with large baits.

These three styles are effective for reaching, holding and dragging bottom. They are most effective in cobble and clean sand bottom, but will become fouled easily in places where algae and other debris collect.

My favorite jig head styles for fishing in shallow waters up to 50 feet with moderate winds and tides are the Banana and Stand Up Jig heads. Another style of jig head that I like looks like an upturned boxing glove and is called just that—the Boxing Glove. There is also a Horse or Pony Head Jig which has a turned down nose and a spinner blade that—like the Banana, Boxing Glove, and Stand Up heads—is designed to skim along the bottom, making it less liable to pick up junk while drifting. All these styles max out at about 2 ounce weights so they are not going to be heavy enough to be effective in deep waters, especially when the drift is fast and large bulky baits that add lift are added.

The Stand Up style head as well as the Boxing Glove and Banana Heads plant themselves on the bottom with the hook sticking up straight, making it easier for a fluke to take the hook if it should grab the jig while it is standing still on the bottom.

The beauty of these shaped heads is the fact that when rigged with a Plastic Squid Strip, real squid strip and fish of some sort, Fluke Sandwich style, they will readily skim along the bottom, relatively snag and debris free with a very squid like, natural action that fluke absolutely love.

FLUKE JIG DRIFT RIGS

The next logical step in the evolution of fluke rigging is simply a variation on the original sinker drift rig theme, a jig drift rig. Essentially, it is a double hook rig that replaces a static sinker with a baited, working jig, that functions to get the entire rig to the bottom as well as catching fish. Simple to rig and use, this "double fluke sandwich" is my personal favorite overall set up for fluke. This method is most effective in waters from the surf break to about 60 feet, or even deeper if the drift is not so fast that the rig is pulled off the bottom too quickly.

There are several reasons for favoring multiple hook rigs. First of all, having two baited hooks down there will double your odds of taking a fish right from the start. On top of that, if two rods are fished with this double hook drift rig, there are four hooks down there working. When fishing alone or when the boat is holding a consistent drift attitude, it is possible to fish a third double hook rig from a "dead stick," a rod that is being held in a rod holder.

My daughter Julie with two different five-pound fluke she caught in 40 feet of water off Fishers Island on a basic drift rig—a jig with soft plastic Mario's squid strip teaser, six inches up to a three way swivel, then four or five feet back to a teaser, with both hooks baited with a strip of real squid and a live minnow bait. The double fluke sandwich rig.

I personally don't like "dead sticking," because without being able to detect the strike as soon as it takes place, the fluke will often swallow the hook and be seriously damaged. If that fish is short, it must be thrown back dead or dying and that's a waste of a valuable resource.

For this reason, drifting with an unmanned rod, though effective, should not be practiced unless all the fish in a given area are "keepers" or fishing is so very, very slow and that the additional line is needed for scouting purposes. A double fluke sandwich drift rig can be tied up with many different droppers off the main rig. The basic set up that I have found to be most effective is tying the main jig (functionally a working sinker) with 6 inches or less of 20 to 30 pound test mono to a three way swivel. Then cut five or six feet more of 10 to 20 pound test mono or fluorocarbon and tie that to the dropper or trailer hook. By using a lighter pound test on the longer dropper hook, more expensive jigs can be saved should the dropper become snagged. Some people like a shorter dropper line, but I feel that the extra length allows the dropper to skim closer to the bottom, plus if a fluke misses the jig, being so far back, the delay gives the fish enough time to recover and take a second shot at the dropper bait. This situation often catches a fish that would have been missed with a single jig or short lined dropper.

It is a good idea to use a loop or swivel to attach the jig, so they can be easily changed, as tides increase or decrease in speed, which would mean changing jigs to always maintain that "minimum weight" necessary to reach and hold the bottom. I don't use swivels too often because they can pick up debris that would drop off a plain line, plus they are another piece of gear to replace, when rigs are snagged and broken off. Always employing the minimum amount of weight required to touch and drag bottom adds a degree of sensitivity to this set up that will always help catch more fish. I tie a good knot, usually my version of a double improved clinch knot, to the dropper hook which is not changed no matter how big a jig is used to get it to the bottom.

The main jig should always be the minimum weight required to reach and drag bottom under the prevailing tidal conditions. Normally, due to the additional lift and drag from the dropper line this jig is normally between ⅜ ounce and one ounce to fish less than 40 feet of water. Bait the jig with a Mario's Squid Strip, strip of cut squid and if the jig is small enough, a live or dead fish of some sort. But I don't always put a fish on the jig in these double hook set ups, especially when using a large jig with a heavy wire hook, besides, it is not necessary unless there is bait to spare. When deep fishing the jig is essentially a working sinker while in shallow waters it will catch perhaps 20 to 25% of the fish, usually the larger ones on a given outing.

The dropper hook should be size 2/0 to 4/0 to minimize hooking smaller fish. I prefer a Lunker City Texposer Hook, though circle hooks will work as well. The dropper hook can be as simple as a plain hook baited with a real squid strip and a mummichog Arkansas shiner, or a fly of some sort baited this same way.

The best dropper rig I have found so far is to slide a 2 inch long, Luhr Jensen, day glow, B-2 "popcorn squid" on the line before tying the hook, slip one to three beads on the line to act as spacers and to prevent the plastic squid from slipping down on to the hook, then bait as described above. The day glow color is activated by sunlight and glows an eerie, ghost like whitish green color in the dark. Down in deeper, darker waters, it appears to draw the attention of the fluke over other, non-glowing colors.

When drifting with a rig of this sort hold the rod tip up slightly so it meets the line at a near 90-degree angle. This provides additional feel and sensitivity when it comes to detecting the often light take of a feeding fluke.

Fishing with a dropper rig is not as sensitive as using a single jig tied straight to the line. The additional drag from the dropper line will dampen the feel of the jig somewhat as well. However, if you rig up to a stiff, light and sensitive rod as described in the tackle chapter, and spool with a no-stretch Fireline or some other light super line, it is possible to deter-

Netting fluke that obviously hit the dropper rig. Having a baited dropper drifting a few feet behind a jig is a one-two punch that often hooks fish that miss the jig.

mine just what's going on down there by simply learning how various strikes and taps from things on the bottom feel. It's a skill that can be learned with experience.

When using a light stiff rod with Fireline or 20 pound Whiplash or Spider Wire Stealth, which are as thin as 2 pound mono, I can differentiate between the bottom types, detect the instant any junk is picked up by a hook, and easily distinguish the pull of a squid or crab from the bite of a fluke, porgy, or other species that may be encountered. This sensitivity adds a degree of fun and satisfaction to this style of fishing that is lost when heavy, clunky gear is used.

When a fluke hits the jig, because it is essentially a straight attachment to the line, a hard strike is felt and the hook should be set immediately. I usually point the rod quickly to the water, reel any slack line up immediately and set the hook as soon as weight or resistance is felt.

When fluke take the dropper line, they appear to approach from behind and suck it down, often "chewing" their way up the bait as they go, so it takes some practice to detect the strike immediately. From the business end, the angler holding the rod will feel either a "lightening up" of the entire rig as it drifts, a softer "tap tap" or possibly just the sensation of some added weight, as the fluke grabs hold of the trailing dropper rig and is dragged or swims along with the drift as it tries to swallow the bait.

This is why one should only wait a second or two before setting the hook on the dropper and set instantaneously when a hard smack is detected on the jig. Otherwise fluke that are short may become gut hooked. Better to miss a couple strikes by reacting too fast, than to kill fish by not reacting in time to prevent the fish from swallowing a hook down into its esophagus.

This method hooks most fish in the mouth or lips, without deep hooking very many potentially short fish. A strike on the jig is always a hard hit, due to the straight connection between it and the rod tip. When they take the dropper, due to the connection and extra line off to the side, the take is not so hard and sharp, though with practice it can be detected immediately.

The dropper hooks can be modified with Spin and Glow spinners or spinner blades in front of the B-2 Squid that are designed to add flash to the rig. I prefer to keep it plain for two reasons. Spinners add more weight and snag more. They also add more drag and dampen feel even more, plus when a rig is snagged and lost the financial loss is greater.

Obviously, it is a good idea to tie up rigs in advance. When a loop set up is used to secure the jig, do not add the jigs until they are ready to be baited and dropped into the water. There are a number of leader management systems out there. I have tried many and none is perfect. The best thing, if possible, is simply to tie them and hang them up in a safe place so they can be easily reached when needed. More practical is a simple zip lock bag, with a tied rig that is coiled and held firmly in two or three places with twist ties. This is as good a system as I have come across for keeping pre-tied fluke drift rigs separate and neat in a tackle bag. Cut twist ties in half to be more efficient and tie rigs as you go. Storing them over long periods during the season will often cause rust on the cheap metal of ties that can stain and just plain look bad. I tie rigs up in advance and keep them at home, only bringing along what is needed for a given trip. The stuff to tie new rigs is always in the boat in case the pre-made set ups run out.

Over the past 20 to 25 years this "double fluke sandwich" drift rig set up in various configurations has been the most successful fluke producer for me in waters less than 60 feet in depth. Remember, when seriously fishing I use two rods, one with a right hand reel, the other with a left hand reel. There are keel lock attachments for "Fish On" rod holders all around the perimeter of my boat, so I can move the holders around as needed and one is never very far away.

When a strike is felt on one rod, the other is placed securely in a holder, while the first fish is hooked and landed. While playing the first fish, I watch the tip of the second rod as much as possible. If it dances or bends over I reach over quickly and pull hard on my no stretch line to set the hook and leave that rod unless it appears to be a bigger fish than I am reeling in, then I do a quick switch up or hand a rod off to the nearest person.

Very often this double hook rig will take a fish that bites the bait off the jig, then takes the dropper hook as it drifts past a few seconds later. This is a common occurrence. Proof is in the fact that you generally feel a hard strike as the fluke whacks the jig and misses the hook. Then five or ten seconds later a second strike or tap tap is felt on the dropper line. I know this is the same fish, because it often has a piece of soft plastic or bait that was torn from the jig in its mouth when the hook is removed. Proof positive the benefits of using a double fluke sandwich rig.

Using two rods is also a great way to test out variations in rigging and baits. Use the standard on one rod and something different on the other. Sometimes the second rod is a totally different rigging than the first, sometimes its merely a different colored jig or teaser. Point is, this makes it easy to fine tune rigs, by seeing which one works best, then switching all the rigs on the boat to the "color" of the day, or what ever combination of things is working best.

DOUBLE JIG RIGS

The final variation of the fluke jigging set ups, is to tie up two jigs in tandem, one a short distance above the other. Although at first look this appears to be much like a drift rig, this rigging style is actually quite different. Tandem rigging is a method that I personally do not employ very often because it requires constant jigging, which is a physical strain on my hands, which have been weakened by operations for carpal tunnel syndrome. Plus the double jig set up is difficult to use with two rods and I really like doubling my odds with the double fluke sandwich rig as described above.

However tandem jig set ups have been proven to me as possibly even being better and more productive than my "double fluke sandwich" style drift rigs, by Mike Adams, a locally known and proven fluke catcher. Mike's technique and abilities are backed up by the fact that he holds the

Connecticut State record, the largest doormat recorded in Connecticut since the state began keeping saltwater fishing records back in the 1980s. His catch was a monster 14.5-pound doormat he caught back in 1989. Mike's record is in the "Off Shore Category," which means that it is a fish that was caught by a Connecticut angler who leaves and returns to a state port, but caught his record fish in waters of an adjacent state such as Rhode Island or New York. Mike caught his fish off Misquamicut Beach in about 30 feet of water using a tandem jig rig, which is his trademark method of fluking.

I have had the pleasure of fishing with Mike on numerous occasions, me with my double fluke sandwich drift rigs, Mike with his tandem jigs. On every occasion, Mike caught more fluke than I did, so his success is beyond the realm of luck or good fortune, it has to be his method of fishing. Mike's aggressive style of fluke fishing is simply better. I would do it, but I simply do not have the hand strength required to fish this way all day long like he does.

Mike is partial to pink jigs. Until I fished with him, I would never have tied a sissy color like pink to the end of my line, but the fluke don't think so, they hammer pink (which is basically the color of squid) and Mike has hundreds of big fish to his credit as proof, including numerous contest winners and jumbo fish weighing 10 pounds and more.

To tie a tandem rig, use two jigs of different sizes. The rule of thumb is to use a larger jig tied to the end of the line, to act as a sort of anchor. Then go up the line about 18 to 20 inches and tie a loop, where the second jig, which is roughly half the weight of the anchor jig, is attached to the loop.

I've also rigged a dropper fly or baited hook in this location to reduce the weight, but the second jig seems to work better than a light offering such as a fly or hook and soft plastic combo.

Both jigs are tipped with a Mario's Squid Strip and a piece of pre-cut frozen squid or strips of fluke belly, which Mike prepares prior to the trips and are frozen in small plastic containers, so each person on his boat has their own personal bait container, to save time and work while on the water. Mike does so much fluke fishing, he does not have the time to constantly be catching or buying mummichogs or minnows to add to his set ups, so he keeps his rigs simple, a jig, plastic strip and strip of bait. It works and works very well!

The tandem rig is sent to the bottom, then the rod tip is lifted up, and then lowered back down, while shaking the rod tip the entire time. This causes the smaller jig to pop and hop around, slightly above the bottom, while the larger, "anchor jig" is dragged along, lurching forward or off the bottom slightly with each flip of the rod tip. It is a proven fluke killing technique.

Tandem jig fishing is a labor intensive, active and aggressive method of fluke fishing that has proven its worth to me every time I have fished from the same boat as Mike Adams, the man whom I originally started calling "The Fluke Meister" after our first fluke fishing trip many tides ago.

Mike is so hard-core when it comes to fluking that 40-pound stripers could be rolling beside his boat, but he wouldn't reel in a fluke rig to cast to them. On his fore arm he has a tattoo of a fluke with a jig in its mouth and an inscription that says: "Fluking Beautiful. " You gotta love this guy's dedication!

5

FINDING AND CATCHING FLUKE BAITS

LIVE SQUID: THE BEST FLUKE BAIT OF ALL

While drifting for fluke, we are often plagued by other critters that chew up our offerings. Porgies, cunners, and other bait stealers can pose a problem when drifting too near to structure. Crabs, skate and sea robins can easily ruin a trip when they are over abundant, by simply destroying baits when they strike and getting in the way of any fluke that might possibly strike.

However, when drifts are in prime areas and the fluke are being cooperative, schools of squid will often be in the same area. The evidence for the presence of squid are slow, sloppy, pulling "grabs" onto the baits. Squid often attack a bait as aggressively as a fish, some times becoming an annoyance because they are constantly pulling at the baits, giving rookies and those who have never experienced squid attacks the impression they are getting strikes from fish. This will often cause them to set the hook needlessly, ripping baits off in the process.

The telltale sign that squid are down there will be the small, "V" shaped bite marks left in squid and minnows from their parrot-like beaks. Often squid will hold on with their tentacles and ride a bait all the way to the surface before dropping off, or they will dart up quickly from the bottom, then turn off as the bait is reeled to the boat. All these are good signs, because where ever you find squid the fluke are not far away.

Fish of any species always have a readily identifiable and sharp strike, that can even be identified as to the species often times by anglers using light, stiff, highly sensitive rods with no-stretch lines. Because squid swim up to their prey, grab it with their tentacles, hold on and take small bites with a parrot-like beak, there is no sharp strike. The line gets heavy, almost like some debris was picked up. Once a squid has hold of your offerings, as they are reeled up, the line will slowly and sloppily slide from side to the side, as the squid tries to swim off. Usually the squid will let go just as the rig nears the surface and daylight hits their sensitive eyes, so the line suddenly lightens up again. When strange things are happening, check your baits, the indication that squid are around will be those distinctive, triangular grooves and beak marks.

Though distracting, with a little experience it is easy to separate the sharp, "tap-tap" bite of a fluke from the "grab" and pull of a squid.

No matter how aggravating and how badly squid are chewing up your baits, stay in that area, because where there are squid you can be sure there are fluke (and often stripers) there feeding on them. Once in a while a squid becomes

Double fluke sandwich rig: the three way swivel attaches to a short line with a jig baited with plastic strip, a strip of real squid and minnow. The dropper is baited with two real squid strips and a minnow, and a plastic mini-squid.

hooked or entangled and can be brought into the boat. We always try to slip a net under any squid that holds on too long.

Many hard-core fluke meisters even keep a rod rigged with a commercial squid jig (which can be purchased in any tackle shop) to drop down and actively fish for squid when they are present in abundance, so they can be caught on the water and used as fresh bait.

The squid jigs don't have classic hooks, but rather have several rings of fine, short gear-like teeth that get tangled in the squids' tentacles when they grab hold, so they simply cannot let go when they want to. These squid jigs are very effective and even some fun to use when squid are abundant. As with any bait, the fresher it is the better it will work. Fresh squid holds on the hook better than the frozen stuff and apparently smells better to fish because they seem to hit it more readily. Regardless of the means, whenever live squid can be captured, rig them up and send them back down to feed a doormat.

Use an appropriate sized hook or tandem hook rig, stick the squid on and drop it to the bottom, alive and kicking if possible. A fresh live squid is the absolute best fluke bait there is, bar none! On numerous occasions over the years, when we were fortunate enough to catch a fresh squid while on the water fluking, within minutes a big toothy flatfish would be flopping on the deck.

One time, a number of years ago when my daughter was 11 or 12 years old, we were out fluking in a 14-foot Lund aluminum boat, in the protected channels and inlets around the eastern end of Long Island Sound. Our primary fishing grounds were the Mystic River and the drifts in the deeper waters off its mouth, around Ram Island and Groton Long Point.

On this day, Julie and I were doing very well in one of my favorite little fluke holes. It was a small spot about 50 feet by 50 yards, a small hole dug out where the channel cuts into the bottom, as it made a corner on its way out to the Sound.

Because this hot spot was in the main channel, it couldn't always be fished due to heavy boat traffic in and out of the Mystic River. It was nearly impossible to fish on weekends and difficult during the week unless it was raining or foggy. On this day it had been foggy and threatening rain when we first got there, so even after the sun broke through, boat traffic was light because the fair weather boaters had already decided to stay home by the time it cleared.

During every drift, we were both taking one or two decent sized, two to four pound fluke from this tiny hole. We would run back every few minutes laughing and talking about the sheer number of fish that had to be lining the bottom in that spot, for us to be catching so many fish from such a small area.

Our baits were being chopped up by fluke and nipped up by squid. Finally, Julie set the hook on one of those sloppy squid tugs out of frustration, in an effort to catch the culprit and she did. The squid was slowly reeled up and swung into the boat. She was promptly squirted with a good shot of that smelly dark ink that squid employ to confuse predators and to cover their escape when being attacked.

She was mad at that squid and my belly laughing, because I had warned her about the ink. Like most near teenagers, she didn't heed my warnings and paid a smelly price.

After the final "I told you so, " Julie was bent on revenge. She asked me to put it on her hook, half hoping I would get squirted as well, but the animal was dry. She said: "Daddy for what that squid did to my clean shirt it deserves to be chewed up by a great big Joey."

I quickly tied on a jig with a stinger hook to double her odds of latching onto any fluke that grabbed this prime offering. The jig was stuck in near the tip of its mantle, the stinger was sunk into its tough gristly mouth near the base of one tentacle, and the bail was opened, sending the still kicking squid down into about 22 feet of water.

Due to the increasing tide and the additional drag and lift created by the bulky squid on the jig it was more difficult to keep it down on the bottom. As young as she was, experience had taught her to let more line out quickly to keep it deeper. About the second or third drop back, after it settled into the depths of the channel, as it skipped off the sand and cobble bottom, her line stopped dead, the rod arched towards the water and the tip began bouncing in those deep, rhythmic throbs that could only be made by a doormat fluke. The fish even ran a few feet of line off the reel against a loosely set drag.

Julie thought she was snagged, but I knew she was into a monster!

After a few tense and exciting moments as she gently, but steadily pumped and reeled her prize off the bottom, I slid our big "wishful thinking net" under a six and a half pound "Joey" to fulfill her wish.

It was Julie's biggest ever fluke and it was netted it in front of a passing tour boat that runs out of the Mystic River. The guy at the microphone pointed out our catch to the people along the port side of the big schooner and they all gave her a big round of applause.

I wasn't sure if it was the accolades or the big fluke that etched a smile on her face for the rest of the day, but either way it was a trip we still laugh about.

A while later, I managed to net a squid that had been grabbing and chewing on my bait for an entire drift. I did the same routine with a jig and stinger hook and dropped it back down into the depths.

As that squid hit the bottom, I lifted the rod tip to take the slack out of the line and bam, another big fluke was on. This one was as heavy a fluke as I have ever felt on the end of my line in over 35 years of chasing these fish. How big this one was I will never know, because it pulled off about half way up to the surface.

When my rod tip suddenly whipped back, and straightened out after that big doormat dropped the hook, I began dancing and ranting around in the back of our small boat like a maniac, cussing to the fish gods who had put that smile on my daughter's face a few minutes earlier. I just plain lost my temper. It always hurts to lose a fish, but it hurts ten times worse when you know it's a monster. I was mad then and am still mad to this day over losing that potential doormat of a lifetime.

Julie whispered, under her breath, "Dad stop it!" and pointed towards the same cruise ship that was on its way back into the river. This time there was no applause, only quizzical looks on faces that were trying to determine if the idiot that was dancing around in the small boat was hurt or insane.

In fact, it was a little of both. Too many lost "big fish" in a life time and I would be in a straight jacket. It was one of those embarassing moments one must endure. Every time we go fluking Julie has to remind me of that day on the water in Mystic that was etched into both our memory banks as a great fluke trip that was improved by two fresh live squid.

BOTTOM LINE: WHEN POSSIBLE CATCH OR BUY LIVE BAITS FOR USE ON ANY AND ALL FLUKE RIGS!

SNAPPER BLUEFISH

Later in the summer, when every "flavor" and size of prey is available, it is often possible to take advantage of things that pop up near the boat. For instance, in the late July or August, when peanut bunker are generally super abundant, they often draw schools of snapper bluefish or hickory shad to the surface. I always keep a "dink rod" rigged with a small lure of some sort handy to catch these fish whenever they show.

Snapper bluefish make one of the best live baits around. There was a time when I would actually go fishing for them the night before an important fluke outing to catch a bunch for bait. That was back in the 70's when there were few bass and an ocean full of bluefish to play with.

I no longer do that, because snapper bluefish have the potential to grow into such hard fighting game fish that it seems a waste to catch a bunch of babies for hook bait. However, when they show beside the boat the minimal effort required to catch one or two for hook baits is well worth it. Like a live squid, they barely touch the bottom before they are eaten by a fluke that could well be of doormat proportions.

I've caught fluke up to seven pounds on snapper blues that were caught right by the boat while fluke fishing, rigged as described above and sent back down to the bottom on a hook. Its a great bait that I frankly don't use very often any more, primarily because I haven't had them swimming past the boat while fluking like they did a couple decades back when they were super abundant.

Nowadays I'm more likely to take out a small snag hook or a cast net to catch peanut bunker to use as fresh bait. They are not quite as large as the snappers, and don't live very long on a hook, but baby menhaden work very well as hook baits for fluke. They have a great deal of flash, a strong scent and will always attract the attention of what ever happens to be around the area. I have also cast baby bunker successfully for fluke, stripers, blues, and small tunoids, because when they are present in abundance, predators eat these little morsels like popcorn, by the mouth full.

HICKORY SHAD

Hickory shad are a bit large to fish live for fluke, unless you know where a 20-pounder is lurking. However, hickory shad fillet strips work very well as a large profile hook bait for doormat fluke. Hickory shad usually hang around inlets and river mouths from late spring through fall and are readily caught on standard shad darts, like those used to catch American shad during the spring run in May. Simply look for breaking shad on the surface or find schools on the fish finder and cast the jigs into these schools. In many places the hickories will be visible on the surface early or late in the day. Normally, boat traffic puts them down during the day, therefore making them difficult to locate in areas where boat traffic is high.

I usually hook shad fillets that are split in half and tapered towards the back, on a large, plain (no hair) jig head, with a stinger hook that is half the size of the hook on the jig. The line to the second hook is 7 to 9 inches long so it will hook near the end of a shad fillet that could be 7 to 10 inches or more long, when targeting big fluke. Use heavy mono to tie the hook to the jig and insert it an inch or two from the tip of the fillet. However, if you are simply fluke fishing for what ever comes along, the fillets should be shortened to about 4 or 5 inches and can be stuck on the main jig of a "double fluke sandwich rig" in place of a strip of squid and without the fish, because it already smells like fish and has such a large profile. Jigs baited with a long fillet of hickory shad often produce the largest fluke, but the numbers game is usually won by that "fluke sandwich" or "double fluke sandwich rig".

CATCHING FLUKE BAIT

A beach seine is a great investment for anyone wishing to catch their own live bait. Any commercial fisherman's supply store will make them up for a relatively low cost; currently under $100 when floats, weights and poles are added. A small seine is an easy way to catch live mummichogs, peanut bunker or silversides to use as hook baits for fluking. An hour or so before launching, go to a sandy, relatively debris and weed free beach to seine up a bunch of mummichogs and silversides for use as bait. That hour spent getting fresh live bait will be repaid with improved catches of fluke. A good haul of silversides will provide enough bait to freeze for a number of trips. However, because I prefer to use fresh live baits over frozen anything, it is best to pull the net before every trip.

Catching fresh bait before a trip is always good investment, if you have the time to do it. But it has some drawbacks.

The net will be wet, usually muddy, full of algae and other slimy, dirty little things, so storage can become a problem. Generally you won't want to take a wet, stinky net in the boat due to the space it takes up and mess it will leave behind on deck and in the bilge. It can't be left in the car for obvious reasons and if its left out some where, say on the trailer or roof racks to dry, there is a good chance that it won't be there when you come in from your trip, especially when parking in a public launch area.

However, if you have a way to store the net the investment of an hour is time well spent.

Two better alternatives are to keep a cast net in the boat, which I have done for a few years. A cast net can be used to throw over schools of bait that show on the depth finder or are seen near the surface. Often on the way out of a given harbor or launch during the late summer, adult or juvenile bunker will be encountered and either size is worth catching when the opportunity arises.

Peanut bunker don't do well once they are netted and will usually perish in a pail of water, even with some aeration, so count on using them as fresh, but dead, hook baits. The flash and scent of a small bunker is as good a bait as one can add to a fluke rig, so catch them any time and by any means possible when out on a fluke fishing expedition.

POTTING MUMMICHOGS

Fresh live mummichogs are one of the best and most readily obtainable live hook baits for fluke. The best way to maintain a steady supply of them is by setting a minnow trap. Anglers who keep their boats at a marina may be able to simply tie a mummi-pot off their boat and catch bait between trips. Or you can set a trap anywhere you have access to a tide marsh or back bay along the coast.

When I am doing a great deal of fluke fishing I will often buy a mummi-pot and simply tie it off, with permission, on one of the docks at the marina where I launch. The people at the docks are pretty good about not stealing the pot itself, but often since they don't see its owner around, they consider it to be communal property and take the bait as needed, which means I sometime arrive to go fishing and pull in an empty minnow trap. But it is a worthwhile gamble.

Even maintaining and catching mummichogs in a trap has a couple of tricks that are worth mentioning. Bait can be tricky. Common baits like bread or fish parts have drawbacks—bread washes away, and fish parts get pretty smelly. Al Fee of Shaffer's Marina once told me he had the best results in his mummi-pot by baiting them with potato chips. The grease evidently attracted the minnows and the chips hold together much better than bread and don't pollute the pot like a rotten fish skeleton. The potato chip trick is one I use to this day and always seem to work pretty well. If it is impossible to maintain your own mummi-pot or take the time to seine or dip net bait prior to a trip, take out your wallet, let the moths fly away and buy live mummichogs or Arkansas shiners from your favorite bait shop and go fishing. Having some sort of live bait wiggling and flashing as it sends out predator attracting vibrations and scents is well worth the cost it takes to obtain it. Fluke can be caught on jigs or hooks baited with a simple strip of squid or even a soft plastic teaser, but in the side by side taste tests I've made over the years, with very few exceptions, adding a live mummichog to the hook will increase your catch by a factor of 2 to 5.

6

DRIFT FISHING METHODS AND TIPS

Like other marine predatory fish, fluke will concentrate in areas that are swept with strong currents that carry with them a bounty of bait with each change of the tides. They lie in wait in these areas, moving with the tides and ambushing their prey from below, nearly invisible due to their ability to change coloration and markings to fit the background. Whenever you are "prospecting" in a new area, every time a fluke is caught or a series of strikes are felt, pay attention to the exact spot and the general type of habitat. Note the depth, tidal phase, if possible push a set button on a GPS, drop a marker buoy, or triangulate the boat's position by quickly looking around and lining up three different points on shore with some notable object behind or in front of them, like sighting in a gun, to aid in returning to that spot for another drift. You can also monitor the boat's position to any nearby lobster pot buoys

Even take note of the current patterns and slick or rip lines where a fluke is caught and how the boat relates to them as a reference for a short, return drift. In other words, when a fish is caught, use the best available means to note the exact location of that productive stretch of water and keep drifting until the bites stop. Do not leave success to chance—those fish may not be there in fifteen minutes if they are moving with the tides, as many predatory fish do. Work that small hot spot with precise drifts until it dries up. Then using the information you have, such as the depth contour at which those bites occurred, the type of bottom, direction the tide is sweeping, try to find

When in doubt, fish a slick line. Flat water spots like this can mean a current line caused by structure below the surface, weeds, feeding fish, or any number of other things. Something is definitely going on below, and in areas where there is no other structure to look for, stopping the boat on a slick line often pays off in additional fish.

other areas of similar characteristics that may also be holding some fish. This is a focused, intelligent approach to fluking that will help put more of these sporty flatfish in the net.

Successful fluke fishermen look for and pinpoint productive drift zones, then fish them hard using the prevailing current and winds to push the boat through exact, very specific zones where the fish are being caught. If the winds are not cooperating or perhaps the drift is too slow due to slack tide, don't be afraid to turn on the gas or electric motor and use some horsepower to get the boat through the area repeatedly. Not so much here in the north, where anglers are fishing in the open ocean or Sound, but to the south in areas that may be narrow and curvy. Anglers may prefer to troll rather than drift, especially in the South where fluke fishing is done in protected rivers and bays. It is a great way to maintain speed control.

Trolling is a valid method for pin pointing and maintaining drift angles. As long as proper speeds of 1.5 to 3 mph or better are maintained, trolling will work very well for fluke fishing.

Remember: if you find fluke, pinpoint the area and keep fishing it until the fish stop biting. I call it "Rennie's Rule" #1: "Never leave the fish."

LIFTING AND DRIFTING METHODS

Rennie Robinson is a long time friend and fishing buddy. I had the great fortune to be able to fish with him many times over the years and learned many tricks from this sage and experienced multi-species angler. Rennie readily shared his knowledge and techniques with me and anyone else he hung around with.

His knowledge was often imparted with concise, meaningful, and intelligent phrases that I heed to this day, and refer to them in my writing as "Rennie's Rules." They are humorous classic sayings that I use constantly. Another one, that applies more readily to largemouth fishing, but one that I employ to some degree fluking as well: "Never jig a jig."

Rennie always felt that the movement imparted by the act of reeling, along with the tips and rolls of the boat, gave a jig enough action by themselves, so I was taught by him to reel a jig slowly, occasionally lifting to feel for bottom structure and if baited, for the presence of a fish. This is essentially how I work my fluke rigs as they are drifted over the fishing grounds.

The rod is held at a constant ninety-degree angle to the line, occasionally lifting the jig off the bottom and feeling for that "release" or negative "tap" when it touches back down with a weight that may be a little too heavy. By lifting and feeling constantly with a light, sensitive and powerful set up, with some sort of non-stretch line, as previously described, it is possible to feel the slightest take, any unweighting of the line or pulls and pecks from squid and other creatures, as well as when even a slight amount of debris or weed has fouled one of the hooks.

In contrast, when "jigging the jig" by bouncing it radically up and down along the bottom, it will be much more difficult to feel the subtle changes in weight and drag from a piece of weed that can ruin any chances of a strike. By not "jigging your jig, " it is possible to maintain a direct connection to your baits. This dragging and lifting method allows an angler to fish much more effectively, efficiently, and with a higher degree of sensitivity to what is happening down below.

Note that this is the opposite action and jigging method of "Fluke Meister" Mike Adams, who uses a tandem jig set up that he constantly pops and works the whole time he is fishing. Remember, Mike's method only pops the smaller jig, the bottom one drags along, only lifting or lurching forward a small amount with each pop of his rod tip. Try both methods and see which one works out best for you.

MAINTAINING A PROPER DRIFT ATTITUDE

The drift is critical to successful fluke fishing. Not only is the speed and direction of the boat, but also the attitude of the boat in relation to the drift line can play an important role in overall catches for a trip. Any time there are two or more anglers in a boat, the angle at which their lines are maintained during the drift is important. Ideally, the boat should be drifting perpendicular to the direction of the current. This way two or three anglers, who may be using more than one line each, can spread out along the gunnel of the boat so their lines are running parallel to the direction of the drift. This not only keeps lines from fouling each other, but by spreading them out across the boat, as wide as possible for each drift, like a rake, it allows for more thorough coverage of the bottom. If a boat turns so it is stemming the tide and lines all run close together, not only will there be a much greater chance lines will become tangled, the catch may be reduced as well, because they will be running in a much more narrow track or grove.

Often when this happens whom ever is in the front end of the boat as it drifts will often receive the majority of strikes and therefore catch most of the fish. Generally, in my boat we split up a desirable catch equally, so it does not really matter who catches the fish, as long as they are hooked and netted. However, in some cases, such as introducing a kid to fluke fishing or taking out anyone new to the sport, note their position in the boat in respect to the drift and if possible put them on the leading edge in order to increase their odds of taking fish. If the drift is too fast, baits will be pulled up off the bottom by the friction and drag of water on the line and baits.

(A good reason for using light, small diameter, slick, dense lines such as Fireline when fluking.) Too slow a drift and baits may not move fast enough to stimulate these predators into striking, and crabs, skate and other slow moving bait robbers will be pouncing on your rigs.

ELECTRIC MOTORS FOR DRIFT CONTROL

Ideally, when drifting for fluke, the wind and tide should be moving in the same direction, to provide a nice brisk drift that allows lines to hold bottom at an angle anywhere from perpendicular to about 45 degrees to the bottom and be evenly spaced as wide apart as possible. However, when lines run close together tangles will start happening. This is often due to other dynamic factors that are affecting the drift, such as cross currents, winds that change the attitude of the boat, or current lines that curl or swirl, rather than running straight. One simple solution can be shortening drift distances. However, under severe conditions this will not work and the captain must do something positive. Boat attitude can easily be controlled by occasional "kicks" from the gas engine, or better yet an electric trolling motor.

Big primary boat engines do not allow for pinpoint boat control during a drift, but they can be used to kick the boat one way or the other to keep it drifting properly. Many serious marine anglers, particularly fluke fishermen, add a saltwater electric trolling motor to the bow or stern of their boat to allow fine tuning of boat attitude during drifts. Under most drift speeds and conditions an electric trolling motor can be used with very little effort to maintain the boat in at a consistent angle to the tide.

Bow mounted trollers make it easier to maintain the attitude of a boat. However, mounting on the bow means the motor will take a severe pounding every time the seas are the least bit choppy or rough, plus they are constantly being sprayed with salt water in that position. Water penetrates deeply because it is also blown into cracks and crevices from the forward movement of the boat.

For this reason I have been transom mounting my electrics for the past decade. It is not quite as efficient, pushing my 20-foot Lund Alaskan from the stern, as pulling it from the bow. However, the motors and mounts will often last longer, especially if you are "cheating" and using an electric that is not designed for use in saltwater. (A warning: in my experience, electric trolling motors, even those designed for heavy salt-water use, tend to wear out after a few seasons. Consider it part of the ongoing cost of fishing!)

When winds are strong it may be impossible to maintain the boat in that ideal, perpendicular position relative to the drift line, but at least it can be held at some sort of angle that will maintain lines spread as far apart as possible.

LINE MANAGEMENT TECHNIQUES

When the drift swings the boat with the wind, like a compass needle, it will cause anglers' lines to line up in the same "slot" and bad things will start to happen. Even experienced anglers will have tangling problems under such conditions. When winds become too strong for the electric trolling motor to maintain the boat in a desirable attitude, so lines are constantly crossing and fouling with each other, reduce the number of lines out, even if it means sharing rods.

Even under normal conditions, if tangled lines becomes a problem be sure everyone has the same amount of weight on their drift rigs or jigs so one line is not drifting faster or slower than another. If one person does not have enough weight on to reach and hold bottom, their line will lift up off the bottom, drift around and catch other lines in the process. Often simply by making everyone switch to the same type and weight rig, so their drifts are in unison, this problem can be nipped in the bud. Another way to combat fouled lines is to have the lead person into the current use the heaviest weight and give the others progressively lighter sinkers or jigs with the lightest weight that will hold bottom going to the person at the trailing end of the drift attitude.

When maintaining a proper drift attitude becomes too difficult, I often give up and either go fishing for a different species such as striped bass or try to find a place that is out of the wind or where the wind and tides line up in a more harmonious fashion.

PLAYING WINDS AND TIDES

The absolute worst conditions for fluke drifting are when the winds are blowing hard, directly into the prevailing tide. This not only builds up bigger waves that make fishing uncomfortable, but it becomes more difficult to hold lines on the bottom in a parallel fashion. A boat that is rising rapidly three feet or so as each wave passes underneath, will lift lines that far or higher off the bottom should a long rod be lifted, creating a "yo-yo" effect that will greatly reduce the catch. These conditions can be a trip killer, because there is very little that can be done to counteract the effects of wind blowing into the tide, which also pushes lines under the boat and slows drift speeds. If there is still some sort of speed to the drift, this situation can be tolerated and coped with, when experienced anglers are on board. Do something else if you have a bunch of rookie anglers with you or the captain will be sorry and living in "tangle city. "

Watch the Weather Reports

The best way to combat this "wind against the tide syndrome" is to listen to a good weather forecast and combine that with the information in a tide chart to determine a place and time when winds and tide drift will be most favorable. Watch the weather channel on TV or better yet, listen to the marine forecast, to get the predicted wind speeds and direction or call a tackle shop that is on the coast where you plan to fish. Some days when the winds will be too strong, anything approaching 20 mph, you don't want to be on the water fishing for anything, so save the gas and mow the lawn or paint something. However, if wind speeds are not going to be too strong, generally under 15 mph, preferably less than 10 mph for fluke fishing, find out the prevailing direction and check a chart for the tides.

Next look at a chart of the area you plan to fish. Determine the direction and time when the tide will run during the ebb and flooding tides. See if that orients well with predicted wind direction and the topography of the shoreline or areas that you plan to fish. Then plan the trip to coincide with the tide that will best line up with prevailing winds. If it is impossible to line them up directly, a wind that is quartering across but not into the tide will allow for reasonably good drift speeds and direction.

Winds that run perpendicular to the tides are not quite as bad as dead into them, but will usually decrease a day's catch. In this case, rather than drifting quickly in line with the tide drift, the boat will be blown across the tide making a drift that is either angled or perpendicular to the tide if it is weak or letting out.

Fluke orient by running with the tides and will swoop up off the bottom or chase bait slowly from behind and below, nipping at and grabbing baits as they drift. This is why so often, when on a perfect drift with winds and tides running in a line, there will be more bites over all. This is probably due to the fact that the fluke will also seem to chase and follow a bait during a drift, increasing the amount of time it has to get hooked, thus increasing catches even further. When drifting with the tides, either directly lined up or at a quartering or less angle, anglers will generally get more bites and catch more fish.

However, when the boat is being blown across the tidal drift by a wind that is blowing side ways to the tide, especially if it is a high wind, the boat will move across the tide drift in a diagonal direction that may become closer to a 90-degree angle, as the tides slow and wind drift takes over, or during slack tide periods.

These conditions will usually allow the captain to maintain the boat at a drift attitude by turning the outboard motor so it angles into the wind and allow two to four lines to be worked effectively without much fouling. I've noticed over the years that under these conditions, the number of strikes is greatly reduced.

I believe this is due to the fact that when lines are running across the tide, the fluke only get a glimpse of the bait as it passes by and therefore are not as likely to chase the lure as they would be if it traveled straight away from them, like the natural baits they are preying upon. It is probably more difficult for them to follow and maintain a good chase on their quarry with their flat bodies while swimming across a strong tidal current. This is just speculation, but it makes sense.

This is why the drift is everything when it comes to successful fluke fishing. Bad drifts only mean fishing will not only be less productive, it may mean fishing will not be productive at all, if the winds and tides are at odds and at high speeds.

Besides being less productive, it's also a heck of a lot more work for the captain when fishing under wind and tide conditions that will require constant adjustments with motors!

DRIFT STRATEGIES

Most of us have our favorite fluke drifts that we go to and sample whenever we are on the water. Occasionally, the first spot we fish will produce a day's catch in short order. More often, we must do some searching to find the depth and areas where fluke are holding and can be caught. In a new area, it may be necessary to make some long drifts in different locations along the shore, or more importantly at varying depths, in order to locate fish. Once an area where fluke are consistently striking or being caught is discovered, focus on a small zone where the fish are located with short, precise drifts. This will keep baits drifting through the fish as long as possible, while the tide is running and conditions are right. Often there is only a short window of opportunity during a given tide, under a given set of conditions that will allow you to catch the fish you are looking for.

The first drift of the day in a given area is often the longest one for me. During that time I may rig and bait different rods and take mental notes as to where strikes are felt or fish caught, while trying to determine where the largest concentration of fish are holding. You may not always catch every fish that strikes, so when the boat passes over an area that yields two or three strikes, be sure to make a couple of short, accurate drifts through that zone, to help pinpoint exactly where the fish are. I've found over the years, whether its fluke nipping the ends off squid strips or short strikes on eels from striped bass, frequently missed fish usually mean you are in an area with smaller fish. For this reason, if missed strikes are persistent, leave that area and look to find fluke that are large enough to take your offerings. Or wade through the shorts for the keepers that are probably feeding in the same area.

Be sure to note the depth and either take a GPS reading or mark a couple of land ranges, so it will be possible to get back to that exact spot for another drift once the bites slow or stop. If the fish are there and hitting well, the boat will be maneuvered up tide and drifted in one, two, or more short, drifts that may be 50 to 150 yards long, depending on the nature of the spot and how long the fish cooperate.

The point is, when fluke are located even if it is around one out of a string of 20 lobster pots, hammer that spot until the fish move on or stop biting. Some days a small zone that may be only a few yards long and wide may produce the majority of or possibly all of the catch. That's why it is so important to pay attention to exactly where the fish are and pinpoint their location as accurately as possible and then with proper boat handling to maintain the proper attitude with the drift line to maintain your lines in the spot where the fish are with short precise drifts.

My friend Sherwood Lincoln is a master of locating and pinpointing drifts. He does so by using a GPS unit that interfaces with bottom contour maps so he can see the areas, map style and from that information use the winds and tides to make perfect drifts over the places he wants to fish.

If nothing else, by noting the depth at which most bites are coming from, it is sometimes possible to determine a starting point when ever the boat is moved to fish a new area. Simply find that depth of water and use it as a starting point until it stops yielding fish, then change depths from there. Most fishermen will start fishing deeper rather than shallower. If the tide is high or incoming I will break that rule and move closer to the beach from my normal 30 to 40 foot starting drift depth. If the shallow water does not hold fish then the boat is moved out into progressively deeper drifts in 5 or 10-foot depth intervals until some fish are caught.

Don't stay in any single spot very long, unless of course, the fish are biting on every drift. When the tides and winds are right, run around until a concentration of fish are located and use a series of short, precision drifts to harvest your catch as quickly and efficiently as possible. There are days when two to four hours out of a six-hour tide will essentially be spent "searching" to yield an hour or two of "catching." But this process is the nature of most fishing efforts and is actually a fun part of the game, as long as the "catching" begins sooner or later!

Playing the Winds

I always prefer the boat to be moving faster rather than slower over the fluking grounds. But unfortunately, the tide changes every 6 hours, so a perfect wind running with the tide during ebb, will push the wind against the tide during the flood, creating difficult or impossible drifting conditions when the strong winds and strong flowing tides are opposed.

As mentioned previously, wind blowing with the tide is always preferred, but in reality this situation seldom takes place. Most of the time, when fishing the waters of the southern Rhode Island coast, where I do the majority of my fluke fishing, the tide runs along the beaches nearly due east on the ebb and west during the flood tide. Most of the summer, the prevailing winds come out of the south or southwest. This means that drifts are seldom straight, but rather at a diagonal, with the tide pulling the boat east or west, while the wind is pushing it northward at an angle in towards the beach.

This is not ideal, but as long as the winds are less than 15 mph and the batteries are charged for the electric trolling motor, proper drift attitude can be maintained for effective drifts.

At times, when the tide is just starting to move, a strong wind will overpower the boat and push it in a northerly direction straight towards the beaches. The strength of that southwest wind determines at how much of an angle the boat will be pushed off the tide during each drift. There are times when I can use this odd drift to my advantage. Look for one of those shallow, often changing channels that are washed out of the bottom as tides run along and off away from the beach. Often this occurs when the water is pushed out by solid structure such as ledge or jetties. These shallow grooves will often hold fish. A northerly wind makes it possible to drift right up the center or along the edges of these subtle little spots. These places often hold fluke in good numbers, so it is worth fishing them whenever possible and from any angle.

Therefore, when keyed in on a hot zone that is producing fluke, take the wind drift into consideration. Always pay attention to what the boat is doing each drift, something that will change noticeably as tides let out, winds increase or change direction. Use these observations to your advantage.

Fluke, like all other saltwater fish, tend to bite better when the tide is moving. They will often shut off completely during slack tide, which is when I usually plan to eat a sandwich when I am on the water during meal times. But never pull the lines in—if there is even a slight amount of wind, keep the rods in holders and use the wind drift to continue fishing. Watch the rod tip at all times so you can respond by picking up and setting the hook before a fluke has swallowed a hook very deeply. There have been many times when a strong wind drift, trolling slowly with the electric, or even back trolling with the main engine during a dead slack tide, will catch a few fish.

A few years ago my wife Karen and I made a fluke trip to a favorite spot. It is a small cut that drops down abruptly from 26 feet to about 34 feet and back up to 24 feet in about 200 yards. It's essentially a shallow valley or trough, between two plateaus. It's a great little zone to drift in.That day we planned to fish the ebb tide in order to take advantage of the westerly winds predicted for that afternoon, so we got there right around high slack tide, which happened to be noon hour, and we were both famished.

There was no tidal movement when the motor was cut, but the boat was drifting with the winds, which were fairly brisk, around 10 to 12 mph that day.

As my wife unpacked our grinders I set her line. Before she got our drinks out of the cooler, a 4-pounder was bending her rod tip towards the water.

I dropped her fish in the live well, hit the switch to fill it with water and my rod was doing the same dance with an even larger fish in the 5-pound class. We took the time to fish while they were hitting and ate an hour later, after the bite abruptly stopped when the increasing wind speed changed the nature of our drift, to crossing rather than aligned with the tide, so our hot bite was ended prematurely.

An hour of wind drifting produced the majority of the fish, including four fish over four pounds in our catch that trip. If we hadn't been paying attention and had a plan, we would have missed that short, intense bite and that trip would have been an average to below average outing, rather than the excellent outing it turned out to be.

Winds of less than 10 miles per hour are easy to cope with and have little negative effect on fishing. In fact, when the wind is running in the same direction as the tide, it will usually increase drift speed just enough to improve the fluke catch and reduce the catch of slower bottom dwellers. In a situation where this level of wind blows across the tide, slight adjustments will be necessary to maintain a proper boat attitude. Under these conditions, it is possible to turn the stern of the boat into the wind and motor down into the water to provide drag, so the boat maintains a constant attitude towards the wind, which can be adjusted by changing the motor's angle into the wind. The hydrodynamic shape of the motor acts like fletching on an arrow to maintain stability and attitude.

When the wind is 15 mph or higher and blowing in the same direction as the tide, fluking becomes more difficult and impossible at some point just over 15 mph or so because the drift is too fast. A drift anchor or two can be tied to the windward side of the boat to slow the drift.

A single drift sock should be tied near the center of the boat to keep it in an attitude that is perpendicular to the drift, so anglers' lines will run parallel and not get wound together. Use the angle of the motor to fine-tune the boat's angle to the drift. Boat control is often better, especially under higher wind conditions, by tying one drift anchor to the bow and another to the stern, in order to maintain drift attitude and reduce speed. This reduction in drift speed when the wind is howling with a ripping tide can make the difference between catching and just fishing.

That point was hammered home many years ago one windy afternoon off the Pink House, a famous local spot at the south end of the Rhody coast. My fishing buddy and I were just learning the intricacies of the south shore beaches and were having a tough time catching fish that day due to a drift that was much too fast.

There is a hole in front of this landmark that usually holds some fluke. It is popular because it's frequently mentioned by name in local reports and easy to find—how many pink-roofed houses are there along the southern Rhode Island beaches? We had been fishing unsuccessfully further to the east and had only a couple of small fish caught during slack tide to show for our efforts. On our way back towards the launch, we saw a few boats in front of the Pink House. One of them was netting a fish as we passed, so we pulled up-wind and began a drift. We sailed almost straight into the beach with that very strong south wind.

Instantly our lines were straight out from the boat with baits flapping uselessly some where in the water column, feet above the bottom zone where the fluke were holding. We looked over and that same boat was netting another fish as we zipped past it at a high rate of speed.

Next drift they were netting a third or fourth fish as we blew by like they were anchored up, but they weren't. Our boats were similar in size, weight and profile, so we were initially wondering what our problem was, until we noticed two taught lines, one off the bow, the other off the stern tied to drift anchors that had slowed their drift to a brisk but fishable rate of speed.

We tied a couple of five-gallon pails to ropes and dragged them in the water. The winds were so strong they had little effect and after seeing them net another fish as we passed them like Parnelli Jones, we pulled up our lines, hauled the buckets in and gave up, nearly fishless for that windy day on the fluke fishing grounds.

You can bet every trip since that day there is a pair of drift anchors on board my boat at all times.

BASIC SEARCHING METHODS

Fluke appear to migrate into an area, then move around within that area, in response to the tides and bait movements, like stripers or bluefish, but to a lesser degree. Bass and blues will often move through an area, pushing bait in the process, while fluke seem to move in and stay.

When drifting the beaches, anglers usually start looking for fluke deep early in the season, in at least 50 to 60 feet of water. Later in the summer, when the peanut bunker are abundant, I often start my drifts in 10 to 20 feet of water, just beyond the surf break because that's where the food is. The fluke will push these little fish into the beaches to feed, just like bass and blues.

Fluke fishing trips are usually a search-and-destroy mission that should be started at a given depth of water, normally whatever depth you left them at during a recent outing or according to what they tell you at the bait shop. Use either as a starting point if no better information is available. Then take drifts either deeper or shallower from that starting depth, in five to ten foot intervals, depending on how steep a drop off gradient you are fishing in a given area. During the summer months most fluke fishermen will be catching their fish between 30 and 60 feet of water. These are comfortable depths that most anglers can fish effectively under most tidal and wind conditions.

I have always believed that when a concentration of squid has been located, a concentration of fluke has also been located. The problem is that neither species shows up very well on depth finder screens so it is usually necessary to fish structure that will hopefully hold the squid and ultimately a concentration of fluke. Many times when we were catching fluke at a steady rate, there have been very thin lines near the bottom that I believe are fluke that have risen up off the bottom and are moving with the tide. The fact that all we were catching in those instances were fluke is all I have to go on for this insight. The point is, while running slowly or drifting, watch the fish finder and look for thin scratchy lines near the bottom that could be an indication that fluke are present and moving down below.

Large concentrations of squid show up like clouds on the screen. If they are not densely packed enough to mark on the fish finder, remember to feel for those tell tale squid bites, which are not sharp like the "digg-digga-digga" take of a porgy or distinctive, "tap-tap" of a fluke. The line becomes heavier and may slide from side to side as the squid grabs the bait and tries to back off with it. If these distinctive squid takes can not be detected due to heavy gear, check baits for the small "V" shaped bites they remove from what ever they attack. The point is, if you are being harassed by squid, or marking schools of squid on the fish finder, stay in that area, unless there

Me with a five-pound fluke that hit a large jig used to fish deep water (80 feet) during the mid-summer slow period. Note the dropper line hanging in front of the fish. Often the larger fish take the jig while the run of the mill stuff is hooked on the smaller dropper rig.

are absolutely no strikes from fluke, because the odds are there are or will soon be some fluke down there feeding on those squid.

When searching for jumbo fluke or at times when these fish move into deeper waters, so more lead must be added to drift rigs, it simply becomes too difficult for many anglers to reach and hold bottom effectively, so their catches drop off to lower levels. Many of the larger fish, but not all, are caught in 80 to 120 feet of water, with many falling to hard core fluke fishing experts who specialize in catching jumbo doormats.

Use maps combined with depth finders and personal knowledge to initially find the places where fluke are feeding. These locations will often change with the tide, but a good place to fish for fluke will consistently hold fish from year to year, so pay attention where fish are caught and drift over those areas repeatedly until the action slows. Remember the tidal phases when the fishing is productive in a given place and try to hit that same spot on subsequent trips, during the same tidal phase.

Along major stretches of beach look for areas that are slightly deeper than the surrounding bottom. Drift over any holes, channels or trenches that are present. Drift parallel and close to humps, reefs, or ledges just off the shore because they can be fluke magnets. Fluke will often be lying in wait over the edge of a hump, waiting for bait to be carried over their position so they can attack. Fish the slopes and bottom of any drop off whether it's leading away from the beach or is a channel edge.

During the course of the summer fluke will initially feed heavily on schools of sand eels and squid, their two favorite food items. However, later in the summer after other species have spawned and their young are concentrated in shallow inshore areas, fluke (generally the medium to smaller individuals) will frequently move in close to the surf break and well up inside coastal bays and rivers to take advantage of the easy pickings.

In estuaries fluke will move up and down river with the tides following the same general feeding patterns as bait and the striped bass and bluefish that follow them up-river and out into shallow flats with the flood tide, and back down river and into the channels and holes with the ebb.

Huge concentrations of peanut bunker moving southward along the beaches during the late summer and fall will attract schools of fluke along with the bluefish and stripers that most people associate with this rich late summer food source.

During this time fluke will follow juvenile bunker schools for miles up inside brackish coastal rivers. Every year anglers catch fluke while chunk fishing for bluefish at least five miles

Mike Green holds up one of 78 fluke that he and I caught in 5-10 feet of water early one fall in the Thames River. These fish were seven miles inside the mouth of the Thames River feeding on peanut bunker. Think shallow late in the summer and early fall for fluke.

from the ocean, up inside the Thames River, located in south-eastern Connecticut. At times this and other rivers will hold large concentrations of fluke feeding on baby bunker that can provide some very good action.

After realizing that shallow water is often the place to look for late summer fluke I had promised myself that when the reports of keeper fluke started coming in from Buoy 27 on the Thames River I would invest a day in fishing the river to see just how many fluke were around and how difficult they would be to catch.

The reports started coming in one year when the Thames was chock full of peanut bunker from Norwich to New London. I launched in Montville and began drifting in the channel with little success at first.

After a little while we saw some peanut bunker twinkling on the surface out over a large sand bar that averaged five to seven feet deep. There didn't appear to be any bluefish on them, so it was safe to drop a small jig down to probe for fluke.

Sure enough, our first drift yielded a couple of short fish. Same with the next drift and every one after that. As long as we were drifting in or near the juvenile bunker schools we hauled the fluke in hand over fist.

At one point just to take a lunch break my partner and I dropped anchor over the top of this sand bar to take a rest.

I had a rod in a holder that had a Luhr Jensen B-2 squid jig baited with a strip of squid and mummichog just skimming the bottom in five feet of water. It was there for about two minutes before the rod tip bent double under the weight of a three-pound fluke.

I wrapped my grinder back up and began fishing again, but using a different double rod method. One rod would be cast with the small baited jig a distance from the boat and across the strong outgoing tide. A second rod would be cast behind the boat and retrieved slowly up to the boat.

I would watch the first rod and set the hook as soon as the line either twitched or stopped drifting down stream. Occasionally I picked up junk but most of the time, the distinctive throbbing of a struggling fluke was felt at the other end of the line.

During the peak of the day's fishing I could only fish one rod because I deep hooked a couple of fish on the "dead stick."

It was a great deal of fun. In the somewhat turbid waters of the Thames River we could not actually see the fluke come up off the bottom as I could when I fished some of the cleaner, shallow water ocean fishing sites over the years.

But once the jig got near the boat in four or five feet of dropping water, the day-glow colored two-inch long B-2 Squid could barely be seen in the murky waters. I would watch it intently as it neared the boat and set the hook when it suddenly disappeared from site.

My partner was working one rod by simply dropping it straight down to the bottom and moving it slowly up, down, back and forth. When the fluke hit he would lift them into the boat "cane pole style. "

It turned out to be quite a day during which we culled a six fish limit of fish between 17 and 21 inches each and released over 60 other fish, about a third of which were keeper size which at that time was 16 inches. We did catch some real "dinkers." That trip I caught the smallest fluke I have ever seen, a tiny little 8 incher.

The discovery had been made. Now, whenever the winds are howling against the tides in the Sound and the peanut bunker are around, if I want some fluke to eat I simply launch in the lower Thames, find a school of juvenile menhaden and drift my B-2 Squid through them with great success.

During the summer when many different food sources come into peak abundance, fluke like many predatory species are opportunistic feeders that take advantage of any large, easily preyed upon food source.

During the 1970s, before the fluke population was fished to oblivion, I was beginning my career as a fishing writer through a weekly fishing report for the Norwich Bulletin, daily paper. During 1975, the year when the current all tackle world record summer flounder, a monster 22 pound 7 once "throw rug" of a fish was caught, there were three other reports of huge fluke in the mid teen size range being caught in my reporting area. One from Fishers Island, the one from Niantic Bay, the other off the mouth of the Thames River. The one from the island was a 16-pound monster that was caught during slack tide, on a baited drail intended for bluefish. That angler must have drifted well off the rocky reefs that rile up the deep, super fast moving and violent waters of the Race.

At that time in history, adult menhaden were super abundant along the entire coast and every large predatory fish fed on them. Fluke were no different, the other two large fluke, one of 15 pounds the other something like 17 pounds, were caught accidentally on live bunker that were being fished for large striped bass. None of these other fish made it into the IGFA record books.

Even though fluke are essentially bottom dwellers, they will often chase bait well up into the water column for many feet above their realm in the sand and cobble. On more than one occasion, I have witnessed working birds and bait that was dimpling the surface, but without any of the typical "toilet flush" boils that would be made when it was being pushed by bluefish, striped bass or bonito. It was an odd situation that I didn't figure out at first.

On one such occasion we tossed small poppers into the bait looking for and expecting some fun surface action from the schoolie bass that had been so prevalent in the area that day.

Nothing, not so much as a short swirl.

I switched to a Spot Lure, which was about the size of the two to three inch long bunker that was observed around the boat and immediately hooked into a three-pound fluke. My son rigged up the same way and landed another fluke of about the same size in roughly a dozen casts, before this "mini blitz" was over.

In a seminar, big-fluke expert Craig Andrews said he's seen big doormat fluke chase bait to the surface in over 100 feet of water on more than one occasion. Proof these fish are very active when feeding and regularly feed up into the water column, probably more often than we anglers realize. At least a few times every summer fluke chase baits and even strike as they are reeled in to make another drift.

Problem is, as anglers, we can't count on finding them when they are feeding up off the bottom, so we must keep our baits within a few inches of mother earth to consistently be successful in taking fluke. The other incidental fluke catches in mid water will be made due to the good fortune of casting the right lure into the right place at the right time.

The point to be made here is that fluke, though a bottom dweller, can be nearly as aggressive a predator as any striped bass or bluefish, but through its specialized adaptations does so with much less expenditure of energy by ambushing its prey unseen from below.

7

FLUKING AROUND FROM SHORE

There are times during the fall striper migration when the surf fishermen can do nearly as well as their counterparts fishing from boats. Unfortunately, this is not true for fluke. Due to their nature and the fact they don't give themselves away by breaking the surface, though they do occasionally draw the attention from birds, its more of a hit and miss proposition, until a consistently productive shore based spot can be discovered.

Certainly, there are times when fluke come in close enough to reach with a cast from shore. Unfortunately, the vast majority of fluke, especially the big ones, will be offshore in deeper waters, so owning even a small boat is a great help when it comes to catching fluke.

I fished for many years from a 14 foot Lund aluminum boat and made some tremendous catches of fluke, once I learned when and where they were holding in the shallow waters I generally fished from Niantic to Stonington and occasionally up the coast as far as Misquamicut Beach, when it wasn't blowing too hard. Once I graduated to the 20 foot Lund Alaskan I'm running today, the south side of Fishers Island, even Block Island came into range and my catch of fluke improved even more.

However, there are a fair number of anglers who can not afford or simply do not want to own a boat for whatever reason, who have figured out when, where and how to catch fluke from shore.

A great lesson in shore-caught fluke was taught to me nearly 40 years ago, a lesson that did not fully sink in for many years, but it was valuable nonetheless.

I was in my early teens. In my high school years, I used to spend a fair amount of time in Noank and Groton Long Point fishing, clamming and crabbing with life-long friends Donnie and Charlie Oat. I made many of my earliest saltwater fishing trips chasing striped bass with these two guys and occasionally our dads, off the rocks in front of a mutual friends house at Crowells Point at Groton Long Point and off the Bee Bee Cove Trestle.

One Friday evening, I had just arrived at the Oats home in down town Noank for a weekend long stay that I hoped would be full of great fishing adventures.

I got there too late for us to walk to the Mystic River to fish. We didn't do any night fishing in those days, so we were just getting settled as the sun began to set when the doorbell rang.

Out on the porch, beaming from ear to ear was one of their neighbors, a kid name Mike Scroggins, holding the first genuine "doormat fluke" I ever saw, a monster fish of 11 pounds and change, that he had caught from the trestle where we often fished.

In those days we had four basic types of lures for stripers, Gibbs Poppers, Blue Mullet Swimmers, Mirror Lures and Upperman's Bucktails, with no plastic, no bait, no nothing, just the hair. It would be years before we learned about adding pork rind to make the bucktail look more like a squid and the soft plastics we all use today were more than a decade away from being brought to the saltwater.

It seems Mike had seen some birds working over a school of surface-busting stripers that were just out of casting range. He knew those fish were up in the cove with the high tide it would only be a matter of time before they would be moving into the holes on either side of the bridge and eventually passing through the bridge and out into the lower Mystic River with the ebbing tide. These school stripers could usually be hauled out of those deep holes by casting a bucktail out into which ever the hole the tide was running into, and bouncing it up the rubble and rip rap that lined the railroad tracks side of either of these productive areas.

Mike dropped his bucktail down close to the bridge and hit that fluke of a lifetime right on its head. There is a narrow shelf of sand near the abutment and that big doormat must have been lying there slurping down baitfish that were being dragged past its nose with the fast flowing current.

At that time, I had little or no experience with fluke and for years considered his catch to be an accident, because all the people I knew who caught fluke did so from boats hundreds of yards out from shore.

Many years later, when I was married and in graduate school at the University of Connecticut, I was fishing off that same bridge for school stripers in the fall.

I was casting a bucktail with a snapper bluefish as a teaser. The stripers loved them and I nearly always connected when I could catch a couple of these little fish, as they fed on silversides around the bridge abutments during tide changes of late summer and fall.

The trick was to pitch the jig up under the bridge into the tide, so it would be dragged down the steep face of that hole where the stripers laid in wait for incoming prey.

That day, I noticed a loop down deeper in my spool so I opened the bail and began pulling line off to reach that loop, so it wouldn't cause troubles the next time I made a long cast. The baited jig evidently sunk to the depths of that hole and sat there for a few seconds while I straightened the line. As it was lifted off the smooth sand bottom, a fish nailed it hard. Initially I assumed it was a striper but it felt different. Within a few seconds there was a good-sized fluke, probably a 4 or 5-pounder floating near the surface.

Not having much experience with fluke at that time I tried to lift it the ten feet up to the abutment, breaking fluking rule #1: "Never lift a fluke you really want to catch," for the first time. The fish dropped back into the water and swam back into the deep hole.

The best method to fluke fish from the shore is with a small baited bucktail. Rigging them, "fluke sandwich" style, with a plastic teaser topped with bait is important, because baits often rip off when cast, but the plastic will usually stay in place. A Mario's Plastic Squid Strip or salt impregnated soft plastic teaser of any sort will catch both fluke and stripers. Often from shore, because there is not any wind drift to lift lures off the bottom, lighter, smaller and easier-to-use jig head styles can be employed. I recommend using Stand Up and Boxing Glove Style jig heads with a four-inch Mario's Plastic

Squid Strip and topped with a strip of real squid and a live mummichog, just like you would when drifting from a boat. Just be prepared to loose a few rigs to snags when fishing from bridges, jetties and breach ways.

When fishing from shore for fluke picking the right spot will be most important. As when fishing stripers, the best places will be areas where the water is moving with the tides.

Breach ways along the coast that have strong incoming and outgoing tides are always great places to fish for fluke. The best spot will be out near the tip of any structure or in the current where it swings around the corner of a jetty in the back eddy that normally forms in these sorts of places during the ebbing tide when fluke are dragged out or chase bait back out into the ocean or river channel. Same thing with tide swept jetties and breakwalls that stick out off the shore. Fish the outer third to its end, where tides run the hardest, by casting and retrieving baited jigs with soft plastic teasers. Later in the summer fish in and under the schools of small bait fish that will surely be in these areas.

During the late summer, when peanut bunker are so prevalent along the coast, they are often pushed up tight to the surf break and along structure such as jetties, which brings the predators such as fluke and striped bass right onto a surf fisherman's doorstep. In these cases there will usually be some fluke down under those schools of baby bunker feeding, even if there are stripers and blues visibly busting on them near the surface.

As a kid I can remember fishing along East Beach, a mile or so west of the famous Charleston Breachway. We used to picnic on a piece of property owned by one of our neighbors, a great outdoors man named Tom "T.J." Fitzpatrick. He would bring a small boat along and if the breakers were down low enough, launch it in the surf break for his son Dan and me to fish from.

Our orders were to keep every decent sized fluke we caught. We would drift down the beach with the tide and after an hour or so T.J. would drive the truck down to retrieve us, the boat and our catch. The fluke would often be filleted and consumed on the spot for supper, by the adults, who would shove burgers and hot dogs into our hands whenever we requested some food. Not knowing what we were missing we were both happy with the trade, fluke for fishing time in the boat.

In those days we fished with classic fluke drift rigs with spinners and beads baited with strips of squid. We quickly learned that by looking for and fishing in the "dark spots," that we could often see moving along the beach over a white sand bottom. There would usually be some fluke and often schoolie stripers feeding on them, that we could catch. Those dark spots were actually schools of juvenile bunker that would move up and down the beach with the tides. There were often some schoolie stripers, even jumbo bass we could see in those schools that we prized more than the fluke, but seldom caught in the process, due to the specialized rigs we employed.

One day, while we were drifting along the beach, about four waves out from the surf break, I heard Dan stuttering in the bow of our little boat. He normally didn't stutter when he spoke, so I looked to see what had him so excited.

The biggest fluke we caught during these early fluke trips were about two or three pounds and under 20 inches. Danny was looking at a monster doormat fluke that had followed his bait up from the bottom, and stuttering in his attempts to get my attention so I could also see this incredible fish. It was a monster, still the largest fluke I have ever laid eyes on in person. It took up at least three to four times the surface area of the average fish we had been catching, resembling a piece of bottom, larger than a doormat, that had been elevated up to the surface.

I had no idea fluke could grow so large and gained some respect and interest in this species after this monster sunk back to the bottom. I have yet to catch a fluke that was even close to the gigantic proportions of that incredible fluke!

There's always this season.

That was before this species had been fished to oblivion by the commercial trawling fleets during the 1970's and 80's, so there were more jumbos everywhere to catch. The fact is that today, an angler walking the beach could reach that huge doormat and many of the other fluke we caught in those days without casting very far.

When these fish are around, they do come in close enough to cast for from shore, but not all the time and in every place anglers are likely to cast their baits. Fishing around the top of the tide is the key to success. One must, through experience and successes, learn the places to fluke fish from the beach or jetties, but there are many, particularly along the Rhode Island Coast and out off of Long Island in areas where people can gain access to fishable waters.

Four decades later I found myself in nearly the same exact spot along East Beach, Fitzpatrick's old A-frame with the shamrock shingled into the roof was looking a bit bedraggled after years of neglect since it was taken from the family through eminent domain by the state of Rhode Island. This time around I was in a much larger, seaworthy boat casting in to those same dark schools of bait and catching small fluke on nearly every cast.

It wasn't quite like "the good old days," our catch was better, because the small Luhr Jensen jigs baited with squid that we cast into those fish work so much better on the small fluke that run up into the surf break than those clunky old classic fluke drift rigs. That huge doormat was long dead of old age, but I couldn't help but wonder if one of its great-great-grand "off spring" was lurking beneath the slow rolling waves.

Any angler who wants to catch fluke from the surf could walk the beaches during the day, spot schools of baby bunker or other bait late in the season, and cast into them with small baited jigs and do very well on fluke. The odds are they would not take many big doormats, but it would almost certainly be possible to cull a couple of legal sized keepers out of a days catch. When the peanut bunker are abundant inshore, this method could be just as effective, if not more so, than casting jigs into the current off a breachway or jetty.

The late summer period of often super-abundant bait sets up a number of possibilities for anglers who fish from shore. Anglers catch fluke to five or six pounds at night under lights off docks around marinas in the mouth of the Thames River. The lights evidently attract small bait, which in turn draw in fluke and of course other predatory species such as stripers and even weakfish in some areas.

Later in the summer, when everything that swims moves into and out of salt ponds and rivers chasing bait, it is also possible for shore based anglers to catch fluke by drifting a small baited jig off a float. During an outgoing tide or with the wind, from the right location, it is possible to cover water for long distances off shore in places with an even and shallow bottom, by fishing like the guy described earlier in the book, who was fishing the small salt pond in Hilton Head North Carolina and catching fluke in four feet of water with a bobber and live mummichogs.

There are numerous other locations where creeks, tide ponds, rivers, and streams flow into the Sound or the lower reaches of large tidal rivers that set up the kind of situation that will attract feeding fluke into shallow waters well within casting distance of shore. These are not the kind of places where anglers are likely to load up, but odds are, there are a few such places that will consistently produce catches of medium to small fluke, beginning in early August when the baby bunker hit the shore, through September or early October, when water temps drop and the fluke begin to migrate out of the region.

In any and all of these shore based fishing scenarios, if you can add a live or freshly dead mummichog or silversides to a jig baited with squid, or fish them alone on a hook, the odds of hooking up will be greatly increased.

8

FISHING WITH "THE FLUKE MEISTERS"

As with any species, catching the oldest, largest members of that population often requires specialized techniques, lures, and fishing tactics. Fluke are no different. Any angler with a line in the water on the fluke fishing grounds has a chance to take a jumbo fish and most who fish hard and often will usually catch their share of fish in the 5-pound plus class fluke during the course of a summer. Though these are very nice sized fluke, they are only the middle sized and slightly more than middle-aged classes of this species. The bench mark size that separates huge doormat fluke from the others is double digits, that fabled 10-pounder, the ultimate accomplishment in fluke fishing.

There is a small but growing cadre of dedicated big fluke specialists who fish deep, with large baits and heavy weights, for the biggest of the big fluke in the sea and they are very good at what they do. There is another group of fishermen who also log in their share of jumbo fluke simply because they are fluke specialists. Anglers who go where the best fishing is at any given time and catch them where ever fishing is most productive, whether it be shallow or deep. Their big fish come through sheer persistence, the numbers game. They fish almost totally for fluke, so over time, by the simple fact that they target this species all the time, they consistently land some large fluke every year.

The guy I refer to in my writing as "The Original Fluke Meister" is a dedicated flatfish specialist, Mike Adams, who targets only fluke and winter flounder. Because their peak seasons do not over lap very much, he can target some sort of flatfish from April through November. If it's flat with two eyes on one side of its head, he's good at catching it. Mike was mentioned earlier in this book (Chapter 4), in the section on using tandem jigs.

I first met Mike in high school. Two decades later, when I was working as the Marine Recreational Fisheries Program Biologist for the Connecticut DEP, Mike called one day to find out if the 14.5 pound doormat he'd caught was a state record and if so, how to fill out the paper work to get recognition for his accomplishment.

At this writing, his fish is still the existing Connecticut state record in the "Off Shore" category, which means it was a fish that was caught out side of Connecticut waters, but in a boat that left and returned to a Connecticut port or launch area. Though a monster fish, I expect to see this record and the current instate record broken at some time during the mid-2000s, as the population of fluke that had been resurrected through strict management efforts during the 1990s, is allowed to mature, age, and grow through protective regulations.

A few years later, I once again crossed paths with Mike Adams when I met and began fishing with Mario Tirone, the inventor of Mario's Plastic Squid Strips. He and Mike were friends, so Mario allowed him to keep his boat and trailer in the yard of his summer cottage at Point Judith, Rhode Island. As a result he, Mario and I try to get out fluke fishing whenever the opportunity arises, which amounts to about once every year or two.

Mike is a skilled and hard core fluke meister, but he is not a deep water specialist, like some of the other big fluke chasers that I know, because he fishes more for numbers than size. However, due to the fact that fluke is essentially the only species that he targets during the summer, due to the sheer numbers of trips he makes and his over all "soak time" on the top notch fluke fishing grounds around Point Judith, Mike manages to catch contest winning class fluke every summer, usually in waters under 80 feet, often under 60 feet.

Another locally (to Connecticut) famous "fluke meister" is Craig Andrews of Niantic. Craig is one of those guys who always seem to have his name on the leader board for the big fluke of the week contest at River's End Bait and Tackle, Saybrook or Hillyer's Tackle, Waterford. I recently realized that many of the largest fluke, numerous impressive catches of ten and near ten pounders that I have heard about while gathering information for my weekly column in the Norwich Bulletin and an on-line report for www.OnTheWater.com over the years, were caught by this highly motivated, highly skilled and aggressive "Fluke Meister. "

Craig has a big fish mentality that he strictly adheres to, no matter what. It's a throw back to his years as a charter captain and rod and reel market fisherman for striped bass. Years back, before the new era of striped bass management, he and a number of other skilled anglers along the coast chased striped bass with hook and line for a living. Craig has paid his dues on the waters of Long Island Sound and knows his home waters around Niantic Bay, out to Block Island, Montauk Point and west to Madison as well as anybody. It's his knowledge of many unknown and unmarked rock piles, reefs, and wrecks that make him such a danger to whatever species he's targeting. Over the last decade that target has been doormat fluke of 10 pounds and more. He is one of the few fishermen I know of who catches top end doormats on a regular basis.

Craig feels that the essence of catching big fluke consistently is being in the right place at the right time, while presenting a large bait in the proper manner to the fish. (Wise words that apply to most fishing scenarios.) He does not take long "blind drifts." Using GPS and or shore ranges, he pinpoints drifts, which are usually made in 80 to 120 feet of water, right on and around specific pieces of structure which may be drop offs, ripples in the bottom terrain, the down-tide side of a ledge, a small reef, or along the edges of some of the larger more famous striped bass and bluefish deep water reefs in Eastern Long Island Sound. Craig also likes to fish the many small deep water holes and ripples that are scoured from the depths of the Sound by tides and strong currents. He feels these small, hard to find pieces of structure concentrate the jumbo fluke that he's constantly searching for.

This Fluke Meister uses heavy Penn fast retrieve reels, stout rods and Power Pro super braid lines of 30 to 50 pound test. He generally fishes with 8 to 20 ounces of weight in order to hold the bottom against raging tides, often for hours, before the conditions get just right and finally allowing him to present his huge baits to his huge quarry.

Generally Craig runs hair teasers held off the front of a large 4/0 to 8/0 hook at varying distances using a series of beads. A few beads so the hook is forward when the fluke are taking well and further back beyond the hair, when they are hitting short.

He's another man who goes by the mantra "Large baits equal large fish" because his large hook is always loaded up with a huge mouthful of meat, which could be a fillet of fluke, sea robin, hickory shad, a whole herring, or if possible a whole fresh live squid, perhaps the best bait of all, though he says he's caught some big fluke on the brown skinned side of fillets, the "flukes" that he removes from the big fish he catches. Remember fluke parts in the boat must be legal size, so these baits are big, at least 17 inches now-a-days.

Bigger fluke like this 8 pounder often come from deeper water and by using large baits. "Big baits mean big fluke" is a credo all the hard core "fluke meisters" live by.

Andrews is totally obsessed with big fluke and dedicates nearly all of his fishing time, effort and resources to catching doormats. He's eternally in pursuit of that currently unheard of 20-pounder, which he knows is swimming around down there somewhere. He says: "Once you start consistently catching big fluke that's all you think about," using himself as a prime example.

I believe some lucky fluke fisherman will catch that elusive 20-pound doormat some day, possibly by 2015, as long as the population of fluke is being sufficiently protected to provide some individual fish with the opportunity to reach their maximum potential size. With sufficient restrictions on all fishermen, commercial and recreational alike, a few old fish will escape each year, eventually allowing a very small number of individual fish to live their entire life so they can achieve weights of over 20 pounds. Most of the existing IGFA line class world records range from the mid teens to the 22 pound, 7 ounce all tackle world record that was caught off Montauk Point, by Charles Nappi, back in the 1975, just before commercial and recreational pressures pushed fluke populations to the brink of oblivion.

I get out on the fluking grounds every so often with Sherwood Lincoln, another dedicated big fish angler who is more broad based at the present time than either Craig or Mike. Craig is a good friend of Sherwood's and they often cross paths while fishing the deep water drifts off Niantic Bay and the other areas they probe for huge doormat fluke.

Sherwood specializes in big fluke and black sea bass, occasionally chasing huge striped bass, which he targeted to the exclusion of everything else back in his market fishing days. Sherwood has caught more than fifty, fifty-pound stripers in his life with his biggest a 63 pound bull bass. He has also guided light line enthusiasts Al and wife Emme Golinski into two line class world records, both 40 pound plus bass taken on 6 and 8 pound test line, during a week's time back in the summer of 1995.

He too has taken this extensive knowledge base and fine-tuned it to help him catch jumbo fluke. Sort of like changing the channels on a TV set, its the same basic input but with a slightly different focus.

During one of my early fluke fishing trips with Sherwood, he was on a mission to get one of us into a ten or near ten-pound summer flounder. We drifted in waters from 80 to 100 feet, targeting edges of drop offs and riffles in the bottom sands in the deep waters of the Sound off the Niantic Bay area and to the west. In fact, that day for a while we were fishing within shouting distance of Craig Andrews. I had not met Craig at that time, so was unaware of the significance of that event at the time.

We spent a few minutes in the morning catching hickory shad, which were filleted for hook baits, to use along with the squid that were also in the bait cooler to sweeten dropper hooks and to add to the shad fillets for color and scent.

That day the winds were blowing hard against the tides, creating miserable drifts, so we had a difficult time managing our lines, but did some how catch eight or ten fish, all over 3.5 pounds. A nice catch, one most fishermen would be bragging about, but unfortunately none of those quality fish was the ten-pounder we sought. The basic big bait, big fish idea worked, unfortunately on that day we simply did not present our baits to a big "mat" or at least not one that was in the mood to eat.

Years back when I was first published in some of the New England regional magazines a very nice and capable charter captain who had read a couple of those articles, offered to give me a lesson in catching big fluke, and invited me along on a trip to "learn a few things about fluking. "

I never turn down a chance to go fishing with experienced anglers for any species. I love talking with and better yet, wetting a line with good fishermen. A great deal of the knowledge and experiences I have soaked in and passed on in my writing has been gleaned from guys like this, who have taken me out on their boats for fishing adventures of all varieties.

It was a friendly challenge so I accepted. I knew his family when I was a kid and had even delivered papers to his aunt. I could tell he was genuinely interested in sharing some of his fluke fishing knowledge and a chance to catch the doormat of a lifetime.

The kiss of death was the fact that he promised that he would show me a 10-pound fluke to photograph, or maybe even catch myself. (Implying, "if I was good enough").

I learned years ago never to guarantee anyone anything, when it comes to fishing. If you want to get skunked, bring along a camera crew, or an important person that you want to impress, and you're done.

This guy fished hard from dawn till dusk. He often set up near many of my favorite fluke drifts, but slightly deeper and with larger baits than I was normally using at that time. In deep water we used drail rigs or large tandem hooks with whole sea herring for baits.

The captain had plenty of photos to back up the stories I heard during the course of our trip. This guy was definitely not a "B-S'er"; he knew exactly what he was doing, except when he promised me a ten-pound fluke. It was a great time and a generally productive fishing trip, minus any true doormats. The biggest fluke was about what I normally catch on a decent outing, in the 4 to 5 pound range.

The high point that day occurred when he stopped the boat at the edge of a deep hole dug by the tides on the outside (seaward side) of Watch Hill Reef. There is a sort of back eddy there, in fairly deep water that I had fished a few times before. It was the same spot that three decades earlier, when there were still come cod around, where an old friend told me he once caught a 45-pound cod.

Knowing it was one of those "big fish places, " I would occasionally drop a jig down there if I was in that area, when the tides were not ripping too hard. He did the same thing, but with the large baits he rigged up I could see how he might just drag a ten-pound doormat from this hole. Because we fished it while the tides were raging it took 8 to 10 ounces of lead to reach and hold bottom with the whole herring that were sunk down to catch that 10 pound doormat.

We hadn't been drifting for long when the captain set back on what appeared to be a heavy fish, judging from the arch in his long stout spinning rod, a bend that could possibly even a be from that ten pound fluke he'd promised—and it was actually closer to twelve pounds of fish.

Problem was, it was in two parts, one from a 10-pound class bluefish that was chewing on a 2.5-pound fluke all the way to the surface. That big chopper reduced his fluke to about half its original size, gave us a thrill and a good laugh in the process.

Big fluke are challenging and difficult fish to catch, even when drifting with some of the region's top "Fluke Meisters. " Anyone can catch a fluke, and many people can catch good numbers of fluke on a regular basis. But only a small group of elite fishermen have the ability and log the time to catch big fluke of six pounds or more and do it consistently.

9

ALTERNATIVE AND INCIDENTAL CATCHES

One of the fun aspects of drifting a heavily baited rig along the bottom is the fact that many species other than fluke are likely to show an interest. Sometimes this can pose a problem, for instance during slow drifts crabs and "the dreaded skate" will latch on to your offerings, wasting time and bait.

However, excluding skate and sea robins, as often as not those incidental catches simply add some fun and spice to a trip. One time Bob Buckley, a friend from my hunting club caught a "barn door" skate that weighed 18 to 20 pounds. That was the only skate in my experience that fooled us because it was big enough to swim around rather than just spin in like the smaller ones do. Until we saw it I thought that he might have a record class fluke.

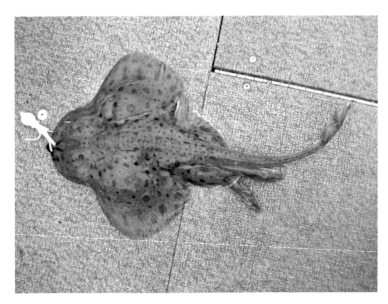

The dreaded skate. When you begin catching these fish more often than fluke the drift is wrong, probably too slow. So do something else until it is right or resign yourself to feeding these annoying fish as long as the boat is drifting too slowly or into the wind.

A few summers back my friends Mario Tirone and John Hillyer, a fluke meister in his own right who owns Hillyer's Bait and Tackle in Waterford with his brother, were on our once a summer fluke trip. We began this tradition a few years ago.

Every summer we pick a date that fits our diverse schedules and we go fluke fishing together, with each outing hosted by a different member of the crew, so each of us has the honor of being "captain" and guiding the trip every third year. Its great fun, a trip I look forward to making every summer.

On this particular day I was the host captain and had Mario and John out fluking on one of my favorite shallow water drifts off the Rhode Island coast.

For some reason that day, it seemed like every time John would ask a question about something, within ten minutes it would happen. For instance, after fishing for nearly three hours he made the observation that we had not caught any trash fish. That drift a sea robin and skate were caught as the ebbing tide let out.

We ate lunch during the slack tide, making some fruitless, skate filled drifts as the boat slowly drifted around with a very slow wind drift as the tide began to build up enough to push its way back towards Long Island Sound.

Once we got a decent drift back, John said: "Do you ever catch porgies off this sandy stretch of beach?"

Minutes later, a cloud of these bait stealers showed on the screen and bam I nailed a big scup shortly after, as we all had our baits "ratta-tat-tatted" to shreds.

This prompted me to move out into deeper waters near a reef that was marked by lobster pots. When John saw the rough bottom as we passed over the reef, he said I bet we catch a sea bass in this spot.

Sure enough, someone came up with a small black sea bass, to keep his uncanny streak intact. At that point I was calling him John "Kreskin" Hillyer.

Shortly after we all had a good laugh about the sea bass, I turned and said to John: "Hey, why don't you ask me if I've ever caught a 10-pound fluke?" Hoping on hope his streak would continue.

He did as requested.

Ten minutes later we were drifting along the edge of a drop off where that reef sinks out into 45 or 50 feet of water. We were moving slowly past a lobster pot, which was chumming up a storm. Earlier we had caught a whiff of the smelly lobster boat, as its owner came in to check and bait his traps, and that was one of them.

Right on cue, I had a jolting hit that if it was a fluke had to be that huge "Joey" that was requested earlier.

As yards of line were ripped off my light bait casting outfit we all knew that I was definitely not hooked into a fluke. Being that it had run so far and hard, without cutting off, we also knew it probably was not a bluefish.

Twenty minutes later we were still chasing that huge striped bass around. I was using the boat to pull it away from pot warp and the reef in order to keep it in open water where I would have a chance to catch and release what was surely a very big striper.

Five minutes later I was disappointed when the line broke. The big fish had not taken the jig, with its double loop of 30-pound mono. It had taken the dropper bait that was tied on with 10-pound test monofilament and it simply could not hold up to the constant chafing from that big fish's sandpaper teeth.

That particular day we caught about every species of fish that one can expect during a day on the water during August, save blackfish and bonito. Catching some of the other species that are not targeted adds some spice to the day and are welcome, especially the larger stripers that would occasionally take a fluke rig. I have caught them to about 20 to 25 pounds and lost a couple of fish larger than that over the years. I've caught weakfish, bluefish, sea bass, blackfish, winter flounder, porgies, even a couple of trigger fish during some of our hotter summers.

Bluefish with their double-edged serrated teeth simply cut rigs to shreds and usually swim off with expensive jigs or dropper hooks in their jaws. When blues become too prevalent I will usually leave that area to avoid them.

Same thing with porgies. Some people will add them to their live well, because they are an edible fish. Personally I don't like to eat them and never take one home to eat myself, even if the fluke are not cooperating.

However I once fished with a guy who loved porgies. When they were present he would put a loop in his line above his fluke jig and add a small snelled hook that was baited with a tiny piece of squid so he could catch those pesky porgies. He was just as happy to fill the live well with these little bait stealers as fluke. Frankly I wish there were more people like him to thin out the porgy population.

The best incidental catches to be made while fluke fishing will usually occur when drifting near a ledge or reef. Blackfish and black seabass frequent solid structure and therefore often take drift rigs and jigs baited with squid as they pass by. A few anglers I know even fish these areas with the intent of taking sea bass, with the occasional fluke.

A problem, particularly inshore, are the porgies that frequent these same sorts of structure. If you are willing to put up with the shredded baits and keep some sort of plastic as teasers, the time spent drifting for fluke near reefs and rock piles will yield some very good eating fish along with an inordinate share of lost rigs due to fouling on rocks and "ghost" lobster pots.

There are times when windowpane flounder become a nuisance on the fluke fishing grounds, especially when fishing in shallow waters under 30 feet. They are a member of the flounder family and for this reason are edible, in fact very tasty, I've filled a couple of large ones myself over the years out of curiosity. Problem is as their name implies they are so thin they are nearly see-through like their name "windowpane" would imply.

During one of those days when drifts are off and the fluke are coming much too hard, don't hesitate to fill out a catch with these paper-thin flounder if large enough individuals can be caught.

Last but not least is the sea robin. At times and in certain places along the fluke fishing coast these fish will literally inundate an area, essentially ruining any chance there might have been to catch fluke. Big mouthed and aggressive they readily gobble down any and all fluke fishing rigs, often long before a fluke has the chance to take one's offerings.

With their huge pectoral fins they have given more than one fluke angler a thrill during the early portion of the fight when they surely thought they were into a heck of a doormat. But with experience they can be distinguished from a fluke, with a darting, pulling fight that lacks that "digga-digga" sort of pull that makes a fluke so distinctive when hooked, due to their flattened body shape.

The huge pectoral fins of a sea robin give them some leverage in the water, with large three pound or so individuals actually making a pretty good account of themselves on light tackle.

In the boat you have to be careful not to be punctured by one of their sharp spines, which make them difficult to handle for many people who can't get past their ugly faces. They don't have very sharp teeth and can be held by the jaw, like a largemouth bass for relatively easy hook removal.

If you can get past the grunting and their ugly face, sea robin fillets are actually not bad eating, much better I think than porgies or bluefish. I have to admit that on a few occasions over the years, on those days when the sea robins were in and taking the baits long before the fluke got a chance, I have taken some large sea robins and filleted them in place of the fluke that I could not catch. If I didn't tell anyone what they were eating no one would complain either.

When the fluke are scarce or impossible to catch, due to the "sea robin factor" keeping a few sea robins can occasionally save the day by providing some decent eating fillets on those days when you made the fateful mistake of promising someone back home you would return with some fluke for supper. Sometimes the promise of a 2-pounder can be just as difficult to fulfill as the promise of a 10-pounder!

10

CLEANING, CARE, COOKING, AND STORAGE

I am a hard core catch and release fisherman who has been releasing fish, all species of fish, even good sized fluke long before it was in the vogue. I seldom freeze any fish to eat, because its almost always possible for me to catch fresh fillets of some sort, pretty much on demand because I am a year round angler.

Not everyone has this luxury, so most fishermen who retain some of their catch for food should develop a system of handling their fish that will provide top quality table fare.

Because we are essentially spoiled, my family and I are very picky fish eaters. I only target a few species specifically for the table and that short list includes off shore pelagics such as tunas, mahi-mahi, mako shark (which as I have grown older and more "delicate" has become a rarity), inshore delicacies that include winter flounder, blackfish, black sea bass, and fluke, plus a few of the best eating freshwater species such as walleye, yellow perch, and bluegills. Of the lot, summer flounder are the hands down favorite.With white delicately flavored flesh, fluke fillets will make literally any recipe a hit. But the key to quality meals of any species lies in how they are cared for from the moment a particular fish is destined for the fish box.

The greatest fish consumers on the planet, the Japanese, will and do eat literally everything in the sea. As a result, they have done a great deal of research into proper methods of storing fish until consumption. In a report that I came across many years ago, it was determined in taste tests that fish that were bled out before they died and immediately iced, were of superior quality and taste to those of the same species that were allowed to die, without bleeding.

In the open oceans, commercial factory ships rapidly process and flash freeze their catches on long sea voyages. Being that I prefer fresh over fresh frozen fish, the best thing to do when a definite keeper fluke is caught is to bleed it out while it is still alive. The Japanese in that article recommended that cutting the tail in the caudal peduncle area (the tip of the fleshy portion of the tail) was the best method to kill the fish, because the fish died more slowly and hence bled out more thoroughly.

I prefer to kill the fish in a more humane manner, with one deep cut through the aorta or heart, that severs that "v" shaped wedge between the two sets of gills at least an inch from its point. They die rapidly but bleed profusely in the process. Allow the fish to bleed itself out, then set it in a cooler on ice after it has died.

The best way to do this is to allow the fish to bleed out in a live well or container of some sort that has some water in it, so the fish does not spray blood around the boat or bruise itself with its dying flops on a hard, often hot deck. Do not allow fish to sit in bloody water for long periods of time either. Be sure to ice them as soon as they expire.

Sounds brutal, and it is. However, for top-notch fillets of any species follow this procedure or some facsimile on any and all fish that are destined for the table or freezer.

Immediate icing is the key to insuring top quality fillets from every fish that is brought home for dinner or to freeze, even if it is not bled out.

Being that I personally don't freeze any fish, except the occasional tuna and then only for a few weeks, I seldom fish for limits of fluke. Most of the time I am only looking to keep two to four fish at a time. For this reason, four to six fluke will stay alive all day long in the live well, as long as they aren't bumped around too much in high seas or left too long in unoxygenated water where they will die quickly.

If fish are bled out into live well water, drain and refill immediately, because any fish that are placed in the tainted water will quickly die. Normally, it will be possible to keep a small number of fish alive and kicking in the 24 gallon live well for an entire trip, as long as the well is occasionally drained and refilled with fresh water or an overflow spout is used. I monitor the catch constantly and usually keep one fish short of what I really want, so I don't have to cull fish that may be stressed, for the sake of conservation and ethics. If I should catch a ten-pounder and I've already got a limit of dead fish, it has to be released by law and by good ethics. No other option is acceptable.

As the catch is monitored, if they look stressed, they will be bled out and packed in a cooler. Otherwise, they will be kept for the entire trip, bled, and packed in ice right in the live well for the trip home, a more efficient method than having to keep a separate cooler full of ice in addition to one that may hold beverages and food for the trip. It is the ice from the beverage cooler that is dumped into the live well at the end of the day, along with another bag or two, if necessary, for a long trip home.

Never leave fluke or any fish that is destined for the dinner table on a hot deck, in a plastic bag or a hot cooler for even a few minutes. At the very least add some fresh, cool seawater in a cooler that is holding fish prior to icing.

When de-hooking your fish try to hold them in your hands with fish gloves if possible so they don't flap and beat themselves up and bruise their delicate white side fillets, by needlessly pounding on the deck. All these details will insure the freshest, best looking, best tasting fillets once they make it to the kitchen.

FILLETING

Fluke are one of the easiest fish to fillet. They don't have any additional bones; their skeleton or "rack" is simply a spinal cord with bones running parallel to each other and horizontal to the ground, with a small rib cage protecting their internal organs.

All that is required to fillet a fluke is a sharp knife with a long flexible blade. I have two sizes, a large 9 or 10-inch blade for large fish and a smaller, 6-inch blade for doing delicate work on larger fish and for use on smaller fish of various species. Regardless of the blade size, knives must be kept sharp at all times, except during the skinning phase. I normally use two six inch knives, for filleting, alternately dulling and sharpening the knives as I go, so after all the fillets have been removed, the dullest knife can be used to separate skins from meat in one single operation.

Commercial fish cleaners fillet a fluke or winter flounder with one single cut on each side of the fish, using a long bladed knife. Each fish is a two cut operation on each side. Starting at the tail, the knife is cut down to the backbone at an angle until the bone is felt, then the blade is laid down flat on the back bone and run up to the head while holding the blade parallel to the spine, with a gentle slicing and sawing motion. Pressure is applied downward on the blade, to hold it on the spine itself but at such an angle, so the blade is riding parallel and it does not cut any bone slices in the process.

Flip the fish over and repeat the process on the other side.

I find it easier to fillet the second side if the first side is just freed up, but not completely removed until after the second fillet has been cut off.

Two cuts total for the fish, not counting the two cuts to split the skin away from the fillet.

The only problem with this method is it takes time to learn well and there is a small amount of meat left in the shallow pocket that lies below the spine, meat that was sheltered to some degree as the blade was run along the spine. It is only a small amount of meat, not enough to warrant the additional time it would take to cut it out for a commercial fish cutter.

However, for someone like myself who only does a few fish at a time, it pays to try to remove every savory morsel of flesh from the rack of a fluke by using a four cut filleting method.

It is slightly more time consuming but with practice allows for the removal of every bit of meat from the ribs.

This method is simple and easy to learn.

Starting on the dark side of the fish, make an angled cut behind the gills in the thickest portion of the "shoulder meat," right down to but not through the spine. Then run the tip of the knife blade right down the middle of the backbone from head to tail, without cutting ribs or into the spine itself. Simply allow the blade tip to touch the spine all the way down, essentially splitting the meat into two portions along that line.

Then, (separately on each half of this top fillet) push the blade down beside the spine until it meets the rib bones, then turn the blade side ways and run it along the ribs and out to the flukes of the fish a short section at a time, using a short, sawing motion. Don't cut the fillets off that first side, but free both halves of the meat off that top side of the fish, from the spine out towards the flukes while taking care not to puncture the body cavity on the belly side of the fillet or shave pieces off of the ribs. When cutting around the ribs, once the flesh has been cleared to the anus, stick the knife through and cut it all the way through to the tail.

It will be easier if the meat is separated under the skin, but the skin is not cut through on this topside along the flukes. Save this final removal step until after the white or bottom fillets have been removed.

Flip the fish over and repeat the process on the white side of the fish, but completely remove the fillets from this side, then go back and slice through the skin that is holding the fillet along the flukes on the top or brown side of the fish.

Once the fillet meat has been removed from the fish, the skin is still attached. It is usually easier to remove the fillets from all the fish being cleaned in one operation, while using a dull knife to remove the skin from all fillets in a second operation. Using a dull knife will minimize the chances of cutting the skin and leaving little patches of skin on the fillets.

To remove the skin, lay the fillet, skin side down flat on the cleaning board or table, so it is parallel and close to, but not hanging over the edge of the cutting surface. (I use the Formica topped leaf of an old discarded dining room table as a fillet board, though any wide piece of clean, smooth, unstained wood will work.) Using a dinner fork and starting at the tail end of the fillet, pin the skin, about an eighth of an inch in from the tail end, to the cutting surface, or simply pin it with a fingernail. Angle the knife blade through the meat gently at a 45 degree angle, until it reaches the skin, then, while still cutting, reduce the blade's angle until it is laying flat on the cutting surface, between the meat and the skin. Now, with the blade laying flat on the board and tip completely through the fillet as it lies flat on the cutting surface, push the blade to the front of the fillet with a gentle sawing motion in one slow and steady motion. Be sure to put downward pressure on the knife blade, which should be running parallel, not angled in the least, to the line of the cutting surface and the meat should peel cleanly away from the skin. If the skin starts to curl or buckle, stop, lay it flat and continue this step.

I know one guy who likes to use the fluke meat and skin for fluke bait, so he cuts them off separately when he fillets his fish and freezes them for bait. Be careful that these pieces are large enough. Technically in my home state of Connecticut, any piece of fluke that is kept on the boat must be of legal size, so unscrupulous people can't fillet short fish on the water and claim they were legal.

If you have the freezer space, wrap up the racks and innards of your fluke, place in two doubled up and separately tied plastic bags and freeze until you make a dump run, or garbage pick up day, unless you are one of those who uses it in a compost pile or for fertilizer. Freezing potentially stinky material until just before the garbage is picked up will mean you won't have to put up with the flies and stench from a garbage can that is holding offal from cleaned fish, or any other meat and trimmings that can rot for that matter.

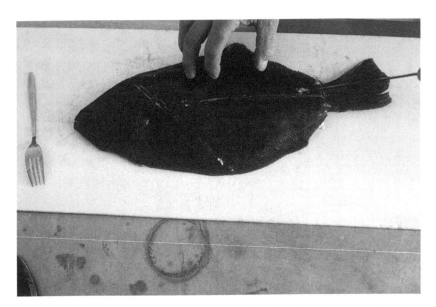

Filleting fluke. First, cut down the center of the spine. It is best to make cuts on both sides of the fluke before removing the fillets, because it is more difficult to make clean cuts with meat removed from one side. (Photographs of filleting by Sherwood Lincoln.)

Cut parallel to ribs to loosen one half of the fillet.

Remove the fillet and repeat on the other half of that side. Turn fish over and repeat on the second half of the fish, ending up with four strip fillets.

Remove the skin from the fillet by laying it down on a table and cutting parallel to the skin. It may be easier to hold the skin using a fork.

LONG AND SHORT TERM STORAGE OF FILLETS

Never wash and immediately freeze fish or it will quickly burn and taint its delicate taste, as the water on the flesh crystallizes in the freezer. I can always tell frozen fish due to the fact it has a slight "fishy taste" that will become stronger the longer the fillets are frozen. That strong taste will be caused immediately in fillets of fish that are cleaned and wrapped wet.

I don't usually rinse saltwater fish fillets that are to be frozen until just before they are cooked unless they are very bloody. The reason is due to the biochemistry of marine fish and freshwater, the cells of the fish will tend to absorb freshwater, thus causing more damage when it freezes due to crystallization. If washing is necessary, pat the fillets dry with a paper towel, before freezing.

In the absence of other better freezing methods it is best to package fish in zip lock bags or double wrap before placing in a freezer.

It is much better to freeze fluke fillets in water, than simply wrapping fillets, even double wrapping. To do this, place fillets in a milk carton full of water, allow the water to over flow, close down the top using clamps or clothes pins and freeze it into a solid block of ice with the fillets in the middle. The carton is easily labeled with a waterproof marker.

Freezing in water was the best way to freeze fish until the advent of vacuum sealers at a reasonable consumer price point. Now it is possible to pick up a Tilia Food Saver at around $100.00, well worth the price for anyone who freezes anything. These things are simple and easy to use. Sealing fish fillets in an air tight bag is far better than a block of ice when it comes to long term freezing. Anything stored in a vacuum-sealed bag will stay fresher and last many times longer. I often vacuum seal fillets that I don't want to freeze, but also don't want to eat immediately. They keep three to five days in the fridge and will taste like freshly cut fillets when cooked. Be sure to dry them well so there is no water or juices in the bag, since it's the liquids and juices that give stored fillets a "fishy" taste.

COOKING

Fluke fillets from a properly bled out and cooled fish are of such high quality and so delicately flavored that they literally make any fish recipe a hit. This is not a cookbook and frankly I don't have very many different recipes for fluke that I cook because they are so good simply fried, baked or broiled that they don't need anything fancy to taste great.

Any fillet of fluke can be cooked in butter, with nothing but seasoning such as lemon and oregano, garlic or whatever suits your taste buds. Those same fillets can be dipped in a mix of egg and milk that are whisked to a froth and then dipped into flour, Bisquick, bread crumbs or even powdered mashed potato and then fried or baked to a delicious golden brown.

Two favorite recipes that are slightly more involved are baked stuffed fluke and fluke tempura.

The tempura is a simple matter. Purchase an oriental tempura batter mix. The trick I've found is when you mix the tempura with water as instructed, do so with ice water that has been strained. The coating should be watery, but thick enough to stick without running off before they can be placed in a bath of hot oil.

Be sure that the oil is up to temperature. Then dip fillets and drop in one at a time. Tempura fluke is one of my favorite ways to eat this delicate white meat. Inside that crisp tempura coating it is a great contrast in textures and flavor from the flaky white, sweet-tasting fluke flesh.

My mom's baked stuffed fluke is a simple recipe that requires a little more preparation.

Use a baking pan that has enough room for two layers of fluke fillets. I usually place fillets in the pan before hand to be sure of the fit.

Then take Ritz crackers, crush them up in a bowl with a spoon or other blunt implement, in a blender or by crunching them up in their sleeves with your hands. Add Parmesan cheese equal to about a third of the amount of crumbs, melt some butter in a pan, squeeze in lemon, season and add this to the crumbs and moisten with milk. Adjust the amount of butter and milk to your dietary needs and taste. The end result should be a mix of crumbs with melted butter and enough milk to make it squishy to the touch, but not runny. It should be of a consistency that it can be easily picked up and molded but soft enough that it would splat if it were thrown against the wall.

Now lay one layer of fillets in the baking dish, cover with the Ritz Cracker stuffing mix, add the last layer of fillets, add a few pats of butter on top, squeeze some lemon (leaving the peels spread out evenly on top of the fillets), and a few dashes of paprika. Place in an oven that has been pre heated to 350 to 375 and cook until the top is brown and the sides are bubbling.

This Ritz cracker mix is an old family recipe that I also use in baked stuffed clams, lobster and crab with equally stunning results. It's simply the best. I seldom order this sort of stuff in restaurants because it's never as good as Mom's home-made blend.

11

MANAGING THE FISHERY

As a baby boomer I have grown up during a very dark period in fisheries history. The technological advances that came out of World War II and subsequent wars has rubbed off on all facets of society, including commercial and sport fishing. Sonar, loran, and now GPS combined with spotter planes and satellite technology, improved gear and fishing techniques has allowed the commercial fleets of the world to find and more completely wipe out whatever species of fish happens to be bringing in the best prices. If that fish also happens to be a popular recreational species, it will be in double jeopardy. If that species is not sufficiently and correctly protected, by means of regulations and quotas on both sport and commercial fishermen, they can disappear in the blink of an eye.

Fluke was a perfect example of this rapid devastation of an abundant and popular species, during the last quarter of the 20th century.

After World War II, the number of commercial boats rose drastically, along with a demand for fish, as Americans became more health conscious. In 1976, the federal government passed the Magneson Act, which functionally expanded our territorial limits out to 100 miles. With specific exceptions, this important piece of legislation functionally booted a good portion of the foreign fishing boats from our shores, leaving a void for American vessels to fill. Within a decade a newer, better equipped, and more high-tech fleet of American commercial fishing vessels was working our Coastline.

Fish from the North Atlantic were the first to show signs of depletion under the withering pressures that were placed upon them by world wide markets. Like dominoes, population after population of commercially exploited species declined drastically. A species would become hard to catch, prices would rise with demand, assuring their ultimate demise before another species would be marketed in its place, and that too would be fished into oblivion. It was a viscious, unstoppable cycle that would not end until most of our commercially valuable species had been all but wiped out.

Commercially important inshore species such as fluke, winter flounder, scup, and striped bass that also had heavy recreational fishing pressures on them, declined even more steeply and rapidly than those that were either of just recreational or just commercial importance. Everything, right down to bait or forage species such as menhaden and squid, were ultimately affected.

During these dark times the balance of our oceans was changed permanently.

The first fish to disappear was yellowtail flounder, an off-shore species. On the east coast, they were followed by haddock, pollock, cod, winter flounder, fluke, striped bass, scup, tuna, billfish, and sharks, not necessarily in that order. Now due to a combination of over harvest and disease even lobster are on the brink of oblivion.

Between 1970 and 1990, many of these species hit rock bottom catch levels along the east coast. It was both sad and disgusting to see this domino effect take place in nearly all of our major fisheries. From a sportsman's point of view, it was like they took the fish right off our hooks.

Initially, there was no sound recreational fisheries data to work with and commercial numbers were not much better, because most of those guys high lined and lied in their catch reports, so there was essentially no truly accurate catch information to go on in the beginning of this new era in fisheries management, that began with the Magneson Act of 1976.

Striped bass was the species that lead the way, because they were in deplorable condition at this time, with both state and federal managers, who had previously been at the mercy of commercial lobbies, were finally given some of the power they needed to enforce the regulations laid out in species-specific management plans that were created during the late 1970's and early 1980's and fine tuned during the 1990's.

There are still many faults and problems with marine fisheries management then as now, but it was a beginning. Though still a long ways from perfection and still with many issues stacked heavily in the favor of commercial interests, the management of the Atlantic coasts marine species has, in general, steadily improved since the late 1980's and into the new century for most species.

One must remember, that neither commercial nor recreational fishermen are monsters bent on the destruction of a species. Part time commercial fishermen and pin hookers (those who fish commercially with rod and reel), I believe should not be in the commercial fisheries realm because there are too many of them. These "part timers" make it more difficult for those who have been vested in the commercial fishing industry for generations to make a good, honest living, due to the competition for a limited resource, especially under the current quota systems on species such as fluke.

The story of fluke here in my home state of Connecticut reflects what happened to our marine fisheries in general, but on a smaller scale than what took place in the major fishing ports throughout the northeast.

Two things combined to nearly destroy fluke stocks along the Atlantic coast. First was the dramatic increase in commercial fishing interest on this species during the 1960's and 70's, after yellowtail flounder, halibut, winter flounder, cod and other ground fish became harder to catch. Demand increased but many of the species that once fulfilled that demand, simply were no longer available because they had already been wiped out by a burgeoning commercial fleet.

Fluke, which had long been a popular inshore species for recreational anglers suddenly became the target of hungry commercial draggers. The result was a devastating and rapid decline.

The second and possibly most significant reason for the demise of fluke populations was the development of, or expansion of off shore winter time, deep water trawling for fluke. Improved location technology, better ships, improved fishing gear and the incentive to fish harder due to higher fish prices, drove the fishing fleets further off shore along the edge of the

Continental Shelf, to fish on wintering grounds that had not been discovered or at least not previously been fished very hard.

During the fall, summer flounder from the Northeast move off shore and south, to the edge of the Continental Shelf in the Hudson Canyon and New York Bight areas. On their way off shore they spawn and then concentrate, in schools of mixed sizes, in these deep off shore areas that were once like sanctuaries. However, after these areas were located, fluke populations were easily decimated using modern satellite location technology and fishing methods, because they were super so concentrated and therefore extremely vulnerable to trawling during the winter.

Where they had previously been fished primarily during the warmer months while they were spread out along the coast, harvest pressures though heavy were limited by the fact that the fish were spread out to some degree. Now they were year round. With the fluke concentrated in relatively small areas on their wintering grounds and essentially lying dormant during the cold weather months, they were "sitting ducks" so to speak. The end result was a very rapid and near total depletion of our fluke population. The winter time devastation of these fish continues today but it is controlled by quotas and closed seasons.

The story of the destruction and rebuilding of the fluke population is illustrated through two sets of Connecticut based data. One is an old Connecticut based commercial harvest report for summer flounder from 1951 through 1978, the other is the historical catch data gathered by the Marine Recreational Fisheries Statistics Survey Results, that can be pulled off the NOAA web site on the internet.

I remember during the early 1980's, when a NOAA (National Oceanic and Atmospheric Administration) report came to my attention, a report that mentioned the discovery of those wintering concentrations of fluke during some of NOAA's own off shore research trawls.

I was talking with a coworker at that time over this matter, after we both read this dangerous (to the fluke) information. Simultaneously, we looked at each other and said: "Now you can kiss those fish good bye." And that's just what happened.

About that point in time, the commercial fluke harvest drastically increased due to increased demand and the species vulnerability to fishing during this relatively new winter off shore fishery. Within a decade, fluke numbers hit their historical all time low levels. A situation that is reflected in the NMFS (National Marine Fisheries Service) Marine Recreational Fisheries Survey Statistics.

One interesting side bar is the fact that during the 1970's, when Connecticut's commercial draggers were asked to voluntarily to maintain trip logs, most didn't do it, or lied about their catches for fear of "Big Brother" and the computer age that was rapidly closing in on them at that time. Problem is this wide spread fear, greed and deceit ultimately bit Connecticut commercial fishermen in their collective asses. Years later, when coast wide, federal mandatory fluke management plans were implemented, those plans required region wide sport and commercial fishing quotas to be established for fluke. These quotas were based on faulty information and essentially their "reporting lies."

Because the quotas were based on under-reported catches, Connecticut commercial fluke fishermen did not receive as large a portion of the allotted quotas as they would have, had they reported their catches honestly to begin with. This is a fact they still bemoan today and fight over with fishery managers in what has been a futile effort to increase their "piece of the pie" nearly every year.

I personally have no sympathy or support for their dilemma, because it was is a direct result from their years of greed, lies, and inaccurate reporting of their catches. It's pay back for their crimes against the resource that went on then and continues to go on today in the form of high lining, which is culling out of big "money" fish in place of smaller less valuable fluke.

Rod and reelers can usually release their catch with little or no damage. When a fluke is pulled up in a net off the bottom from over 100 feet of water they may die due to delayed mortality from damage to air bladders from sudden depth changes, or from being crushed for long periods of time in the bag of deep water trawls under hundreds of pounds of fish. This practice is a huge waste of this valuable resource, so these commercial fishermen can bring their quota back in large, maximum priced fish.

It's just not right for the sake of additional dollars in the pockets of a few!

If you don't believe culling or high lining takes place, stop by any of the commercial fish houses where catches are sold and watch a boat unload its catch of fluke. It's impressive, yet disgusting to see how few small fish are being brought to market.

What happened to the little fish that they surely catch? They were most likely discarded dead or damaged.

Fluke are not like bluefish, which school in similar year classes. Fluke are all mixed up in size and age classes after spawning, so to end up with that impressive catch of jumbo, maximum dollar fluke, the number of fish thrown back dead or dying had to be very high. I've heard from deck hands that there are as many if not more short fluke wasted as there are big fish brought to market. No one is skilled or lucky enough to fill their nets with 4 pound fish every time out—but these commercial trawlers seem to do it all the time.

The resource is suffering as a result of this greed and no one can do anything about it!

If the fishery is in such poor shape that commercial trawlers can't make a living without cheating, between selling fluke, flounder and other species, which they have also over fished, its time to sell the boat and get a day job.

All this is reflected in the Marine Recreational Fisheries Statistics Survey for Connecticut from 1981 through 2002. This data is presented in two different categories, total catch that includes the short fish that would be released, and harvested catch, those fish that are kept by sport fishermen.

This latter statistic for fluke has been greatly influenced since the turn of the new century, by ever increasing minimum size limitations and generally shrinking creel limits. When the limit is increased or catch reduced it shows in fewer fish brought home by anglers, even though they may be constantly catching large numbers of "shorts" in a day on the water.

The total catch (including throw backs) reached its all time peak for the data set from 1981 through 2002, in 1986, with 916,441 fluke caught. A year when roughly 47% of the total catch was reportedly released. In that time period, before fluke numbers bottomed out, the highest harvested portion (keeper fish) of the catch took place three years earlier in 1983, when 567,160 fluke were taken home to fillet by recreational anglers. In 1983 only 14% of the catch was reportedly released.

It is difficult to determine if this low percentage of short fish was due to over harvest of younger year classes, missing year classes due to poor breeding success, or some sort of data handling or sampling error.

Remember, most of those harvested "keeper fish" would average 1.5 to 2.5 pounds, which means a much higher percentage of the catch would have to be thrown back on a commercial boat that was culling for 4 pound minimum sized fish for the market.

See how significant the waste from this practice can be, if all those commercial throwbacks die?

Bearing in mind, that the word got out to "starving" commercial trawlers about the winter off shore fishing potential for fluke during the late 1970's and early 1980's. Also note that recreational fluke catches dropped precipitously from that point. Size limitations were instituted in this period but did little good under the onslaught from greedy commercial trawlers who literally vacuumed most of the entire population of summer flounder from their wintering grounds off the Continental Shelf within a few short years.

The historical all time low recreational total catches of 44,541 and 56,352, with corresponding harvested catches of 28,314 and 17,707 fluke were made during the 1989 and 1990 fishing seasons. In total recreational catch, this was a reduction of about 95% in three or four short years!

This is hard, statistical evidence as to just how vulnerable unprotected fisheries can be when there is a high commercial price on their heads.

Since those dark years, due to increased protection of summer flounder, primarily from commercial draggers, but also from recreational fishermen, catch numbers have raised steadily to 815,084 in 2000, their highest total catch since the fluke population crash, which was followed by a leveling off in total catch numbers to consistent catches in the 550,000 range for 2001 and 2002 and reportedly an increase over this level according to early, but incomplete 2003 information. A positive sign that fluke numbers have stabilized.

In the future, with some fine tuning in the form of regulations this rebuilt population should be maintained in a healthy condition, from this point on, as long as the commercial trawlers are allowed to fish under strict quotas, or the devastation could happen all over again in only a few years.

It should be noted that due to the fact that fluke creel limits have been dropped and sizes increased, during that same time frame, the harvested catch in Connecticut has dropped to a low of 93,366 in 2002 and begun ratcheting up as the smaller fish that were initially protected from harvest by increased length limits, have grow up into "keeper" sized fish during the 2003 and 2004 seasons.

The harvest statistics for keeper fluke that were killed, naturally mirrors the total catch, though due to the fact that there were many missing year classes of fish, primarily in the older fluke that had been devastated by commercial over fishing, combined with changing recreational bag and size limitations, the harvested catch has averaged from about 45% to roughly 85% of the total catch numbers in recent years, with the lowest harvest percentage of 17.1% of the catch taking place in 2002. This low harvest percentage reflects the increase in overall catch, increased minimum lengths regulations at this time and reduced creel limits, not necessarily a drop in fluke abundance.

At the present time, there are still some major problems in managing fluke. Discard and delayed mortality due to culling or high lining on the open ocean fisheries is the single most important and difficult problem fisheries managers have to deal with. This practice is legally and ethically wrong, but there will not be any cooperation from an economically hurting commercial industry, unless there is literally some one who can't be bribed or intimidated, watching over their shoulders, literally every minute of every trip.

The odds are better of us all winning the lottery!

As this book was being completed in the summer of 2004, the few fluke that I have personally caught this year were of a better than normal (for me) average size, running from 18 to 23 inches with about a 60% keeper to short ratio, which demonstrates how through growth, the population eventually catches up to changes in minimum length limits.

This is another indication that more stringent regulations do have a positive and rapid effect on this sensitive fishery, within a year or two of their implementation. Negative effects will show in the same, quick manner.

In doing my fishing reports, since the recovery of the fluke population began in the mid to late 1990's, there has been progressively more "doormats" of 8 pounds or heavier being caught and reported every season.

Based on the recent, steady improvement of catch numbers and more importantly the increase in the abundance of larger older fluke in the population structure, the future for fluke looks bright.

Recreational catches can be easily controlled via size limits, catch limits and closed seasons. However rod and reel anglers should not bear the brunt of regulation, in order to "save" fluke for commercial fishermen to waste through their illicit practices, because no one is watching. Any rod and reel commercial fluke fishing should be governed under the same seasons, length limits and creel limits as the recreational segment of the fishery. Anyone who is properly licensed should be able to sell their catch, but only an equivalent catch, in size and bag limit, to the recreational fisherman in the next boat. There should be no special treatment for a rod and reel angler just because he sells his catch.

The tail is wagging the dog when it comes to evaluating the worth of fisheries. The money put into the economy by recreational fishermen far exceeds the monetary input from commercial concerns, even with ripple down effects.

Recreational fisheries have footed the largest share of the bill for fisheries management since its inception, because there are so few commercial fishermen relative to their recreational counter parts. Yet the regulations and allocation of the resource continues to be slanted in favor of the commercial segment of the industry, an injustice that will probably never be overcome.

Everything does not have to be equal, as long as the bottom line is that all our fisheries must be managed for the benefit of the fish, not the fishermen, whether they be commercial or recreational.

If a business is run into the ground and goes bankrupt, because its owner has taken out too much profit, too quickly, it's his fault, and no one else's, so he alone should suffer the consequences.

The ultimate goal should be to allow a very limited and specific harvest from both factions of this important resource, so fluke are no longer a "knife edge" fishery, one that could crash rapidly, should spawning fail a couple of years in a row, due to conditions beyond the control of biologists and fishermen alike.

In this imperfect world of marine fisheries management, there has been a gradual increase in the overall numbers of fluke, with progressively more older and larger fish entering the fishery every spring. This means there are more doormats out there to breed and for recreational anglers to catch.

If things continue to improve in this realm, I'm hoping that some day even I will have a very real chance to slip my "wishful thinking net" under a ten-pound doormat, during a perfect drift and with a little bit of luck.

INDEX

Adams, Mike, 35, 78, 96, 130
Andrews, Craig, 117, 131
Arkansas shiners, 64

Bait runners, 27
Bait, being chased by fluke, 116; catching, 89; drift, 56, 81
Baitcasting tackle, 24
Baked stuffed fluke, 157
Balint, Joe, 64
Banana jig, 70
Blackfish, 142, 143
Bluefish, 65, 87, 142
Boats, 31–32; rigging for fluking, 37
Boca Reels, 27
Boga Grips, 36
Bonito, 142
Boxing Glove jig, 70, 122
Bunker, 88, 113, 122

Fluke Meister, 35
Fluke sandwich (rig), 66, 71
Fluke sandwich, 122
Fluke, adaptations and behaviors, 19; as predators, 20; doormat, 112, 130; finding, 40; harvest statistics, 168; future of, 169; identification of, 15; population levels, 162; size limits, 167; tails of, 15; wintering, 164
Fluking, deep, 25
Fluorocarbon, 31
Four spot flounder, 16
Free lining, 58
Freezing, fillets, 156

Gloves, fish, 150
Golinski, Al and Emme, 134
GPS, 32, 104, 132, 159
Gulf flounder, 17

Hillyer, John, 140
Hilton Head (SC), 17, 41
Hogchoker, 17
Holding places, 43
Hook, Line and Sinker, 17
Horse (Pony) head jig, 70
Hot Lips jig, 69
Hudson Canyon, 163

Icing, 149

Jaw spreaders, 36
Jetty, 123
Jigs, 59, 69–71, 122
Joey, 43

Killifish, 65
Killing fish, 148

Liepold, Capt. Gil, 9
Lincoln, Sherwood, 104, 134
Line management, 99
Live well, 37, 149
Lobster pots, 50

Loran, 159
Luhr Jensen squid, 67, 74
Lund, 34, 43
Lunker City Texposer Hook, 74

Magneson Act, 160, 161
Maine, Gulf of, 17
Maps, coutour, 104
Marine fisheries management, 161
Mario's Soft Plastic Squid Strip, 51, 65, 67, 80, 122
Menhaden, 40
Microdynema filament, 28
Misquamicut Beach, 79
Monofilament, 31
Motors, electric, 98
Mummichogs, 40, 90, 91
Mystic River, 44, 84

Nappi, Charles, 134
National Marine Fisheries Service, 164
Nets, 35, 38; cast, 88
New York Bight, 163
NOAA, 163
Nova Scotia, 17

Palomar knot, 29
Paralicthys albigutta, 17
Paralicthys dentatus, 15
Paralicthys lethostigma, 17
Paralicthys oblongus, 16
Penn reels, 132
Pink House, 108
Porgy, 51, 68, 142
Power Pro, 29, 132
Provincetown, 53

Quantum Cabo, 27

Recipes, 157
Reels, 26–27
Rigs, double jig, 78; drift, 56; tandem, 79
Ritz crackers, 158